WHO WANTS TO BE A

MILLIONAIRE

WHO WANTS TO BE A

JUNIOR

B☰XTREE

First published 2001 by Boxtree
an imprint of Macmillan Publishers Ltd
25 Eccleston Place, London, SW1W 9NF
Basingstoke and Oxford

Associated companies throughout the world

www.macmillan.com

ISBN 0 7522 1964 2

Produced under licence from Celador International Limited
Copyright © 2001 Celador International Limited

Special thanks to Katherine Arbuthnott, Don Christopher,
Kathryn Ferguson, Rowan Kitt, Katie Matthews, the Quiz Unit,
Valérie Schenowitz, Adrian Woolfe and Jennifer Wynne.

3 5 7 9 8 6 4

A CIP catalogue record for this book
is available from the British Library.

Designed and typeset by seagulls
Printed and bound by Mackays of Chatham plc, Kent

CONTENTS

How to play

Finally a quiz book designed exclusively for all you junior *Who Wants to be a Millionaire?* fans. So, if you loved *Who Wants To Be A Millionaire? The Quiz Book*, *The Ultimate Challenge* and spent countless hours working your way through *The Bumper Quiz Book*, here's your chance to go for that £1,000,000, either by challenging yourself, or inviting your friends round to see who really is the cleverest of you all!

FOR 1 PLAYER

As on *Who Wants To Be A Millionaire?*, the aim of the game is to reach £1,000,000. But before you can even go on to play the game, you must first correctly answer a question from the Fastest Finger First section. You have just 30 seconds to put the letters in the correct order. When the time's up, follow the page reference at the bottom of the page to find out if you can take your place in the hot-seat and begin your climb for the cash!

Once in the hot-seat

Start with a question worth £100 and once you have decided on your final answer (and you're absolutely sure...) follow the page reference at the bottom of the page to find out if you're right. If your answer is correct, you can play to win £200 and start making your way up that famous Money Tree. The page where each money level begins is listed in the answer section.

As on the programme you have three Lifelines to help you on your way to £1,000,000. You don't *have* to use them, but remember, each Lifeline can only be used once, so don't use them if you don't need to.

Fifty-Fifty

This option takes away two incorrect answers leaving the correct answer and the one remaining incorrect answer. The page reference at the bottom of each page will tell you where to look for the remaining answers.

Phone a Friend

If you have a telephone to hand (and a brainy friend!) ring him/her up to help you out. You have 30 seconds (and no cheating please...) to read the question to your friend and for them to tell you what they think the answer is. If there's someone else around, ask them to time your call for you.

Remember, always ask permission before you use the phone.

Ask the Audience

This works in exactly the same way as on *Who Wants To Be A Millionaire?* except we've already asked the audience so you don't have to! Simply follow the page reference at the bottom of each page to find out what our audience thought. But in the end, the decision is yours.

If you answer incorrectly at any time, you are out of the game. £1,000 and £32,000 are 'safe havens', but if you answer a question incorrectly and you have not reached £1,000 then not only are you out of the game but you will leave without a penny! If you have reached one (or both) of these havens and you answer a question incorrectly, then, depending on the stage you have reached in the game, you will leave with either £1,000 or £32,000. For example, if you are clever enough to get to £250,000, but you answer the question incorrectly, then I'm afraid you will leave with only £32,000. If at any point during the game you are unsure of an answer and don't want to risk being out of the game, you can 'stick' at the amount you have won so far and that will be your final score. As you play, use the score sheets at the back of the book to keep a running record of the amount you have won and the Lifelines you have used.

FOR 2–5 PLAYERS

Players should take it in turns at being 'Chris Tarrant' and posing questions to the other contestants. The rules are the same as for a single player (see pages 6-7). If someone reaches £1,000,000 that person is the winner and the game is over. Otherwise, once everyone else is out, the person who has won the most money is the winner.

Are you ready to play? Good. With all that money at stake, we're sure we don't need to tell you to think very carefully before you give your final answer. Good luck and be sure to remember at all times the motto for *Who Wants To Be A Millionaire?* – it's only easy if you know the answer!

FASTEST FINGER FIRST

FASTEST FINGER FIRST

1

Starting with the least, put these words in order of the number of vowels in each.

- A: Precious
- B: Persuasion
- C: Pirate
- D: Poles

2

Put these marine creatures in alphabetical order.

- A: Whale
- B: Jellyfish
- C: Sea horse
- D: Tuna

3

Starting with the largest, put these countries in order of size.

- A: Russia
- B: Scotland
- C: Andorra
- D: France

4

Put these kings of England in alphabetical order.

- A: Richard I
- B: William I
- C: Henry I
- D: George I

5

Starting with the most, put these sportsmen in order of the number of Olympic gold medals they have won.

- A: Daley Thompson
- B: Steve Redgrave
- C: Matthew Pinsent
- D: Jonathan Edwards

Answers on page 265

FASTEST FINGER FIRST

6

Put these breeds of dog in alphabetical order.

A: Dalmatian

B: Pekinese

C: Airedale

D: Bulldog

7

Starting with the shortest, put these sports in order of the playing time that elapses in a standard match.

A: Test cricket

B: American football

C: Rugby union

D: Association football

8

Starting with the largest, put these animals in order of typical adult size.

A: Ant

B: Elephant

C: Rhinoceros

D: Dog

9

Put these words in order to form the title of a TV programme.

A: Wild

B: The

C: Show

D: Really

10

Starting with the smallest, put these modes of transport in order of average size.

A: Jumbo jet

B: Motorbike

C: Skateboard

D: Car

Answers on page 265

FASTEST FINGER FIRST

11

Put these football clubs in alphabetical order.

- A: Newcastle United
- B: Manchester United
- C: West Ham United
- D: Sheffield United

12

Starting with the earliest, put these tennis players in the order in which they won Wimbledon.

- A: Pete Sampras
- B: Pat Cash
- C: Fred Perry
- D: Bjorn Borg

13

Put these phrases in the order they appear in the Spice Girls song 'Wannabe'.

- A: I'll give you a try
- B: Then I'll say goodbye
- C: If you really bug me
- D: I won't be hasty

14

Starting with the earliest, put these films in the order they were released.

- A: Antz
- B: E.T. – The Extra-Terrestrial
- C: The Wizard of Oz
- D: Mary Poppins

15

Starting with the smallest, put these birds in order of average adult wingspan.

- A: Condor
- B: Hummingbird
- C: Sparrow
- D: Barn owl

Answers on page 265

FASTEST FINGER FIRST

16

Put these cities in alphabetical order.

- **A:** Manila
- **B:** Manchester
- **C:** Munich
- **D:** Mogadishu

17

Starting with the earliest, put these pop stars in the order they had their first UK number one hit single.

- **A:** Elvis Presley
- **B:** Britney Spears
- **C:** Elton John
- **D:** George Michael

18

Starting with the largest, put these bodies of water in order of size.

- **A:** English Channel
- **B:** Atlantic Ocean
- **C:** Pacific Ocean
- **D:** Mediterranean Sea

19

Starting with the smallest, put these islands in order of surface area.

- **A:** Jersey
- **B:** Greenland
- **C:** Iceland
- **D:** Madagascar

20

Starting with the earliest, put these inventions in chronological order.

- **A:** Mobile phone
- **B:** Aeroplane
- **C:** Chariot
- **D:** Gun

❓ Answers on page 265

FASTEST FINGER FIRST

21

Put these colours in alphabetical order.

A: Blue

B: Brown

C: Black

D: Beige

22

Starting with the closest, put these countries in order of distance from the North Pole.

A: United Kingdom

B: Greece

C: New Zealand

D: Ethiopia

23

Starting with the highest, put these darts scores in order of points value.

A: Bullseye

B: Double 18

C: Treble 20

D: Double 15

24

Starting with the most, put these animals in order of the number of limbs they possess.

A: Snake

B: Man

C: Spider

D: Millipede

25

Moving from top of the body to the bottom, put these body parts in order.

A: Feet

B: Knees

C: Belly button

D: Forehead

Answers on page 265

FASTEST FINGER FIRST

26

Starting with the least, put these shapes in order of the number of sides they have.

- A: Pentagon
- B: Octagon
- C: Triangle
- D: Rectangle

27

Starting with the oldest, put these members of the Royal Family in the order they were born.

- A: The Queen
- B: Prince William
- C: Prince Charles
- D: The Queen Mother

28

Put these places in order from north to south.

- A: Glasgow
- B: Southampton
- C: Birmingham
- D: Sheffield

29

Starting with the earliest in the year, put these days in the order they occur.

- A: Christmas Day
- B: Valentine's Day
- C: Easter Day
- D: Halloween

30

Starting with the shortest, put these units of time in order.

- A: Month
- B: Century
- C: Decade
- D: Year

Answers on page 265

FASTEST FINGER FIRST

31

Put these items in the order they were invented.

- A: Video recorder
- B: Thermos flask
- C: Television
- D: Cash dispenser

32

Starting with the oldest, put these pop stars in order of age.

- A: Billie Piper
- B: Madonna
- C: Robbie Williams
- D: Tom Jones

33

Put these household chores in alphabetical order.

- A: Ironing
- B: Hoovering
- C: Dusting
- D: Polishing

34

Starting with the youngest, put these types of person in order of age.

- A: Infant
- B: Pensioner
- C: Middle-aged man
- D: Teenager

35

Starting with the earliest, put these historical events in order.

- A: Death of Julius Caesar
- B: Gulf War
- C: Battle of Hastings
- D: World War I

Answers on page 265

FASTEST FINGER FIRST

36

Put these words in order to form the title of a number one single for Christina Aguilera.

A: Bottle
B: In
C: A
D: Genie

37

Starting with the earliest, put these months of the year in the order in which they occur.

A: February
B: December
C: June
D: April

38

Starting with the smallest, put these groups in order of how many people are in each one.

A: Trio
B: Quintet
C: Duo
D: Quartet

39

Put these cities in order from south to north.

A: London
B: Manchester
C: Edinburgh
D: Sunderland

40

Starting with the smallest, put these animals in order of average adult size.

A: Mouse
B: Elephant
C: Rhinoceros
D: Lion

Answers on page 265

FASTEST FINGER FIRST

41

Starting with the largest, put these musical instruments in order of size.

A: Double bass | B: Violin
C: Piccolo | D: Grand piano

42

Put these schools and colleges in order from north to south.

A: Gordonstoun | B: Harrow
C: Rugby | D: Winchester

43

Starting with the smallest, put these sports in order of the size of ball they use.

A: Softball | B: Soccer
C: Squash | D: Cricket

44

Starting with the closest, put these countries in order of distance from the South Pole.

A: Egypt | B: United Kingdom
C: South Africa | D: Australia

45

Put these historical events in chronological order.

A: Columbus discovers America | B: Romans conquer Britain
C: Invention of the car | D: Vietnam War

? Answers on page 265

FASTEST FINGER FIRST

46

Starting with the smallest, put these
dogs in order of average adult size.

A: Yorkshire terrier   B: Great Dane
C: German shepherd   D: Cocker spaniel

47

Starting at 12 o'clock and moving
anti-clockwise, put these times in order.

A: Two o'clock   B: Quarter past nine
C: Quarter to six   D: Half past four

48

Put these root vegetables in alphabetical order.

A: Swede   B: Turnip
C: Yam   D: Potato

49

Starting with the youngest, put these
'EastEnders' characters in order of age.

A: Martin Fowler   B: Phil Mitchell
C: Roy Evans   D: Ian Beale

50

Starting with the earliest, put these politicians
in the order they became prime minister.

A: Tony Blair   B: John Major
C: James Callaghan   D: Margaret Thatcher

Answers on page 265

FASTEST FINGER FIRST

51

Put these words in order to form
a catchphrase of Buzz Lightyear.

A: And

B: Beyond

C: Infinity

D: To

52

Put these types of powder in alphabetical order.

A: Gun

B: Face

C: Washing

D: Talcum

53

Starting with the earliest, put these
devices in the order they were invented.

A: PlayStation

B: Wheel

C: Car

D: Printing press

54

Put these monarchs in the order they reigned.

A: Edward the Confessor

B: Charles I

C: Victoria

D: Henry VIII

55

Starting at 12 o'clock and moving
clockwise, put these times in order.

A: Two o'clock

B: Nine o'clock

C: Seven o'clock

D: Five o'clock

Answers on page 265

FASTEST FINGER FIRST

56

Starting with the smallest, put these fruits in order of average size.

- A: Watermelon
- B: Grapefruit
- C: Cherry
- D: Plum

57

Put these numbers in order to form the year Prince William was born.

- A: 2
- B: 8
- C: 9
- D: 1

58

Put these ways of cooking eggs in alphabetical order.

- A: Poach
- B: Scramble
- C: Fry
- D: Boil

59

Starting with the smallest, put these bags in order of average size.

- A: Handbag
- B: Sleeping bag
- C: Tea bag
- D: 30 gram crisp bag

60

Starting at the feet, put these items of jewellery in the order they would traditionally be worn on the body.

- A: Earring
- B: Necklace
- C: Anklet
- D: Tiara

Answers on page 265

FASTEST FINGER FIRST

61

Put these characters from
'Dawson's Creek' in alphabetical order.

- A: Joey
- B: Pacey
- C: Jen
- D: Dawson

62

Starting with the earliest, put
these kings in the order they reigned.

- A: Henry VIII
- B: Canute
- C: Edward VII
- D: John

63

Starting with the shortest, put these
time periods in order of length.

- A: Hour
- B: Second
- C: Day
- D: Minute

64

Put these words in the order
they appear in a Christmas carol.

- A: In
- B: Manger
- C: A
- D: Away

65

Starting with the smallest, put these
bodies of water in order of average size.

- A: Ocean
- B: Pond
- C: Puddle
- D: Lake

Answers on page 265

FASTEST FINGER FIRST

66

Put these words in order to form the title of a Disney film.

- A: The
- B: And
- C: Lady
- D: Tramp

67

Starting with the bottom layer, put these items of clothing in the order they would be put on.

- A: Waistcoat
- B: Jacket
- C: String vest
- D: Shirt

68

Starting with the smallest, put these nutshells in order of average size.

- A: Coconut
- B: Walnut
- C: Pistachio
- D: Hazelnut

69

Put these members of the cat family in alphabetical order.

- A: Tiger
- B: Cheetah
- C: Puma
- D: Lion

70

Starting with the thinnest, put these types of pasta in order of average width.

- A: Vermicelli
- B: Tagliatelle
- C: Lasagne
- D: Spaghetti

Answers on page 265

FASTEST FINGER FIRST

71

Starting with the earliest, put these times of day in order.

A: Noon

B: Dawn

C: Dusk

D: Afternoon

72

Starting at the outermost edge, put these colours in the order they appear in a single rainbow.

A: Orange

B: Green

C: Yellow

D: Red

73

Put these mythical creatures in alphabetical order.

A: Pixie

B: Goblin

C: Elf

D: Leprechaun

74

Starting with the fewest, put these competitions in order of the number of different events in each.

A: Decathlon

B: Pentathlon

C: Heptathlon

D: Triathlon

75

Starting with the earliest, put these greetings in the order they would be said through the day.

A: Good afternoon

B: Good night

C: Good evening

D: Good morning

Answers on page 265

FASTEST FINGER FIRST

76

Put these letters in reverse alphabetical order.

- A: Q
- B: W
- C: M
- D: E

77

Starting with the earliest, put these Roald Dahl books in the order they were first published.

- A: The B.F.G.
- B: Fantastic Mr Fox
- C: James and the Giant Peach
- D: The Twits

78

Starting with the fewest, put these creatures in order of the number of letters in their name.

page 25

- A: Cow
- B: Canary
- C: Caterpillar
- D: Camel

79

Put these phrases in the order they appear in the nursery rhyme 'Little Boy Blue'.

- A: In the corn
- B: In the meadow
- C: Fast asleep
- D: Blow your horn

80

Starting with the largest, put these boxes in order of traditional size.

- A: Horsebox
- B: Shoebox
- C: Telephone box
- D: Matchbox

Answers on page 265

FASTEST FINGER FIRST

81

Starting with the highest, put these body parts in order.

A: Skull

B: Shoulder

C: Shin

D: Stomach

82

Put these members of the Royal Family in the order they were born.

A: Prince William

B: Prince Edward

C: Prince Harry

D: Prince Charles

83

Starting with the lowest, put these values in order.

A: 30 minus 21

B: 12 multiplied by 10

C: 33 divided by 11

D: 50 percent of 50

84

Starting with the largest, put these countries in order of area.

A: Kenya

B: Argentina

C: Belgium

D: China

85

Put these words in the order they first appear in our national anthem.

A: Queen

B: Gracious

C: Long

D: Noble

Answers on page 265

FASTEST FINGER FIRST

86

Starting with the lowest answer, put these sums in order.

A: 6 x 2

B: 6 − 2

C: 6 ÷ 2

D: 6 + 2

87

Put these UK cities in order from north to south.

A: Plymouth

B: Newcastle

C: Liverpool

D: Bristol

88

Starting with the earliest, put these literary characters in the order they were created.

page 27

A: Oliver Twist

B: Othello

C: Harry Potter

D: Robinson Crusoe

89

Put these countries in reverse alphabetical order.

A: Turkey

B: Afghanistan

C: Zambia

D: Poland

90

Starting with the earliest, put these historical events in order.

A: Battle of Waterloo

B: Magna Carta sealed

C: World War I began

D: Great Fire of London

Answers on page 265

FASTEST FINGER FIRST

91

Put these words in the order they first appear in the nursery rhyme 'Baa, Baa, Black Sheep'.

- A: Dame
- B: Little boy
- C: Master
- D: Wool

92

Starting with the nearest, put these cities in order of their distance from London.

- A: Sydney
- B: Hong Kong
- C: Paris
- D: Rome

93

Starting with the earliest, put these Harry Potter books in the order they were first published.

- A: The Prisoner of Azkaban
- B: The Chamber of Secrets
- C: The Philosopher's Stone
- D: The Goblet of Fire

94

Put these British cities in order from south to north.

- A: Manchester
- B: Bournemouth
- C: Glasgow
- D: Birmingham

95

Starting with the fewest, put these numbers in order of how many times the letter E appears in each.

- A: Seventeen
- B: Three
- C: Eleven
- D: Ten

Answers on page 265

FASTEST FINGER FIRST

96

Put these foods in alphabetical order.

◆A: Marzipan

◆B: Marmalade

◆C: Marshmallow

◆D: Marrow

97

Starting with the fewest, put these pop groups
in order of how many members are in each.

◆A: Steps

◆B: S Club 7

◆C: The Corrs

◆D: Atomic Kitten

98

Starting with the earliest, put these
queens in the order they reigned.

◆A: Anne

◆B: Victoria

◆C: Elizabeth I

◆D: Cleopatra

99

Put these fruits in alphabetical order.

◆A: Melon

◆B: Pineapple

◆C: Orange

◆D: Nectarine

100

Starting with the lowest number,
put the answers to these sums in order.

◆A: $4 + 4$

◆B: $4 \div 4$

◆C: 4×4

◆D: $4 - 4$

Answers on page 265

50:50	☏	👥

15	**£1 MILLION**
14	£500,000
13	£250,000
12	£125,000
11	£64,000
10	**£32,000**
9	£16,000
8	£8,000
7	£4,000
6	£2,000
5	**£1,000**
4	£500
3	£300
2	£200
1	◆ **£100**

1 ◆ £100

1

Which of these would you wear on your wrist to tell the time?

A: Look

B: Listen

C: Watch

D: Learn

2

Who is Cinderella's friend in the pantomime?

A: Popper

B: Zip

C: Velcro

D: Buttons

3

Which of these animals does not jump or hop?

A: Kangaroo

B: Flea

C: Grasshopper

D: Elephant

4

'She sells seashells on the seashore' is an example of what?

A: Teeth trembler

B: Lip locker

C: Gum grinder

D: Tongue twister

5

Which of these might you find on a car?

A: Sunroof

B: Windroof

C: Snowroof

D: Rainroof

50:50 Go to page 241   Go to page 253   ? Answers on page 265

6

A dairy is concerned with items made from which product?

◆A: Potatoes   ◆B: Milk

◆C: Paper   ◆D: Apples

7

Which of these is a popular toy?

◆A: Heady bear   ◆B: Teddy bear

◆C: Steady bear   ◆D: Ready bear

8

Where on the body might you find a beard?

◆A: Hand   ◆B: Face

◆C: Foot   ◆D: Back

9

Which of these people helps you to cross the road?

◆A: Bubblegum man   ◆B: Gobstopper man

◆C: Lollipop man   ◆D: Peardrop man

10

Which of these is a Muppet character?

◆A: Mr Froggy   ◆B: Mrs Horsey

◆C: Master Donkey   ◆D: Miss Piggy

 50:50 Go to page 241   Go to page 253   ? Answers on page 265

1 ◆ £100

11

Which of these is a popular game at parties?

- A: Pass the postcard
- B: Pass the parcel
- C: Pass the e-mail
- D: Pass the letter

12

What is the surname of the US President?

- A: Tree
- B: Bush
- C: Hedge
- D: Plant

13

Where would a man wear a moustache?

- A: Under his arm
- B: Above his lip
- C: On his shoulder
- D: In his ear

14

Which of these creatures has scales?

- A: Goldfish
- B: Sparrow
- C: Fox
- D: Cat

15

What is the term for a person who looks after children while the parents are out?

- A: Babystander
- B: Babycroucher
- C: Babysitter
- D: Babylounger

50:50 Go to page 241   Go to page 253   ? Answers on page 265

1 ◆ £100

16

Which of these containers is also a part of the body?

◆A: Chest ◆B: Bowl
◆C: Tin ◆D: Pot

17

Which letter of the alphabet sounds like a vegetable?

◆A: B ◆B: D
◆C: P ◆D: T

18

What is the term for an elephant's nose?

◆A: Trunk ◆B: Chest
◆C: Case ◆D: Crate

19

What is the response to this old joke?
'Doctor, doctor, I keep thinking I'm a pair of curtains.'

◆A: Next please ◆B: Take these pills
◆C: Say 'aah' ◆D: Pull yourself together

20

Which of these is not an ocean?

◆A: Pacific ◆B: Amazon
◆C: Atlantic ◆D: Indian

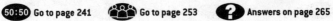 50:50 Go to page 241   Go to page 253   **?** Answers on page 265

1 ◆ £100

21

Which letter of the alphabet
sounds like a part of the body?

A: D

B: G

C: I

D: Q

22

What are the traditional targets in
the fairground stall known as a 'shy'?

A: Turnips

B: Cabbages

C: Coconuts

D: Eggs

23

Which of these animals can be described as a 'gee-gee'?

A: Dog

B: Cow

C: Sheep

D: Horse

24

What type of museum is Madame Tussaud's in London?

A: Clockworks

B: Fireworks

C: Waxworks

D: Gasworks

25

Which of these would you be most likely
to put under your pillow when it falls out?

A: Fingernail

B: Tooth

C: Hair

D: Eyeball

 50:50 Go to page 241   Go to page 253    ? Answers on page 265

1 ◆ £100

26

Which of these is found in tins?

A: Wheated beef   B: Corned beef

C: Barleyed beef   D: Strawed beef

27

What was the title of the 2000 sequel to '101 Dalmatians'?

A: 101 Poodles   B: 102 Dalmatians

C: 1001 Dalmatians D: Puppies and Puddles

28

Which of these would you find on a man's bicycle?

A: Crossbar   B: Annoyedbar

C: Angrybar   D: Furiousbar

29

What is the typical sound made by an owl?

A: Quack   B: Hoot

C: Cluck   D: Honk

30

Which of these is an organ of the human body?

A: Lambney   B: Kidney

C: Calfney   D: Foalney

50:50 Go to page 241   Go to page 253   **?** Answers on page 265

1 ◆ £100

31

What name is given to a year that contains 366 days?

- **A:** Jump year
- **B:** Bound year
- **C:** Skip year
- **D:** Leap year

32

Specifically, what would normally be offered in a school canteen?

- **A:** Food
- **B:** First aid
- **C:** Pottery lessons
- **D:** Football tuition

33

Which of these breeds of dog is famous for its spots?

- **A:** Dalmatian
- **B:** Great Dane
- **C:** Irish wolfhound
- **D:** Red setter

34

What is the fifth month of the year?

- **A:** October
- **B:** March
- **C:** August
- **D:** May

35

Which fictional schoolboy attends the Hogwarts School of Witchcraft and Wizardry?

- **A:** Billy Bunter
- **B:** Harry Potter
- **C:** Martin Fowler
- **D:** Jonny Briggs

50:50 Go to page 241   Go to page 253   Answers on page 265

1 ◆ £100

36

Which family lives in Buckingham Palace?

- A: Lighthouse Family
- B: Addams Family
- C: Partridge Family
- D: Royal Family

37

In the Bible, who was Adam's companion in the Garden of Eden?

- A: Eve
- B: Elizabeth
- C: Edna
- D: Elspeth

38

Which of these might you be presented with as a prize in a competition?

- A: Sunsette
- B: Marmosette
- C: Rosette
- D: Upsette

39

Which city is the capital of England?

- A: Cardiff
- B: Edinburgh
- C: Belfast
- D: London

40

What is the occupation of James Bond?

- A: Footballer
- B: Wizard
- C: Secret agent
- D: Writer

50:50 Go to page 241   Go to page 253   ? Answers on page 265

1 ◆ £100

41

Which term describes something extremely alarming or frightening?

- A: Hair-raising
- B: Nose-elevating
- C: Ear-escalating
- D: Eye-hoisting

42

William is the first name of which of these writers?

- A: Shakedagger
- B: Shakesword
- C: Shakeshield
- D: Shakespeare

43

Which of these is traditionally eaten with chips?

- A: Blancmange
- B: Jelly
- C: Cake
- D: Fish

44

What title is given to the leader of the British government?

- A: President
- B: Prime Minister
- C: Attorney General
- D: Grand Vizier

45

Which of these can follow 'sweat', 'night' and 'tee' for types of clothing?

- A: Trousers
- B: Coat
- C: Shirt
- D: Socks

 50:50 Go to page 241 Go to page 253 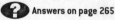 Answers on page 265

1 ◆ £100

46

'Bring It All Back' was a UK number
one hit single for which pop band?

- A: D Club 5
- B: F Club 6
- C: S Club 7
- D: H Club 8

47

Which of these are slices of
fish covered in breadcrumbs?

- A: Fish legs
- B: Fish arms
- C: Fish fingers
- D: Fish toes

48

What name is given to a young duck?

- A: Cygnet
- B: Chick
- C: Gosling
- D: Duckling

49

Where in the USA did the cowboys
traditionally fight against the Indians?

- A: Wild West
- B: Scary South
- C: Extreme East
- D: Notorious North

50

Which of these words does not mean a success?

- A: Triumph
- B: Victory
- C: Achievement
- D: Disaster

 50:50 Go to page 241   Go to page 253   ? Answers on page 265

51

How many are there in two dozen?

A: 12
B: 16
C: 20
D: 24

52

Which of these is a large tractor used for moving rocks and earth?

A: Bullsleeper
B: Bullnapper
C: Bulldozer
D: Bullsnoozer

53

Which of these would you wear to help you see better?

A: Chinas
B: Plastics
C: Woods
D: Glasses

54

The word 'moggy' is used in relation to which type of animal?

A: Badger
B: Gazelle
C: Hippo
D: Cat

55

Which of these comes after 'bubble' and 'chewing' to make two types of long-lasting sweets?

A: Jelly
B: Toffee
C: Mint
D: Gum

50:50 Go to page 241   Go to page 253   ? Answers on page 265

1 ♦ £100

56

'Genesis' is the first chapter of which book?

- A: The Bible
- B: Yellow Pages
- C: Spot the Dog
- D: The Hobbit

57

Which of these would a man go to if he needed his suit altering?

- A: Baker
- B: Butcher
- C: Grocer
- D: Tailor

58

The 'shin' is located in which part of the human body?

- A: Arm
- B: Leg
- C: Head
- D: Chest

59

Which of these is a game in which a ball is hit over a net with the hands?

- A: Jolleyball
- B: Trolleyball
- C: Volleyball
- D: Dolleyball

60

What type of transportation was the ill-fated Titanic?

- A: Bicycle
- B: Car
- C: Ship
- D: Plane

50:50 Go to page 241　　Go to page 253　　 Answers on page 266

1 ◆ £100

61

Which of these is a Scottish dance?

A: Highland toss   B: Highland fling

C: Highland chuck   D: Highland lob

62

Buzz Lightyear is a character in which of these films?

A: Toy Story   B: Games Console Story

C: Football Story   D: Bike Story

63

What does sea water taste of?

A: Salt   B: Cheese

C: Chocolate   D: Strawberries

64

Which legendary creature is half woman and half fish?

A: Dragon   B: Mermaid

C: Unicorn   D: Anthea Turner

65

Which religious leader lives in the Vatican?

A: The Pope   B: The Hope

C: The Rope   D: The Slope

50:50 Go to page 241   Go to page 253   ? Answers on page 266

1 ◆ £100

66

On which of these would you
hang your clothes out to dry?

A: Washing line

B: Railway line

C: Starting line

D: Telephone line

67

In the fairy tale, who climbs up
the beanstalk to the giant's castle?

A: Jack

B: Jeff

C: Jeremy

D: Jimmy

68

Big Bird lives on which of these streets?

page
45

A: Coronation Street

B: Quality Street

C: Wall Street

D: Sesame Street

69

Which of these fruits is generally not red?

A: Strawberry

B: Cherry

C: Lemon

D: Raspberry

70

Which of these might you suffer
from after drinking a fizzy drink?

A: Hiccups

B: Hicsaucers

C: Hicspoons

D: Hicplates

50:50 Go to page 241   Go to page 253   ? Answers on page 266

1 ◆ £100

71

What is the highest mountain in the world?

A: Snowdon
B: Everest
C: Ben Nevis
D: Scafell Pike

72

Which of these is a type of dance?

A: Disco
B: Cocoa
C: Play dough
D: Heigh-ho

73

Which of these would you be most likely to use to clean your teeth?

A: Toothpaste
B: Toothglue
C: Toothgum
D: Toothcement

74

Knight, queen and castle are all pieces in which board game?

A: Draughts
B: Ludo
C: Chess
D: Cluedo

75

Which of these comes in a packet and could be ready salted or cheese and onion flavoured?

A: Crisp
B: Crackle
C: Crumble
D: Chew

50:50 Go to page 241   Go to page 253   ? Answers on page 266

1 ◆ £100

76

Paris is the capital of which European country?

- A: France
- B: Greece
- C: Germany
- D: Italy

77

Which TV talent show is hosted by Matthew Kelly?

- A: Suns in Their Arms
- B: Stars in Their Eyes
- C: Moons in Their Ears
- D: Mars in Their Mouths

78

Which of these animals can describe a neat line of children going for a walk?

- A: Shark
- B: Scorpion
- C: Crocodile
- D: Lion

79

Which country shares its name with a bird traditionally eaten at Christmas?

- A: Bulgaria
- B: Romania
- C: Turkey
- D: Egypt

80

Which of these is a set of breathing and relaxation exercises?

- A: Yoga
- B: Yoghurt
- C: Yokel
- D: Yodel

50:50 Go to page 242 Go to page 254 **?** Answers on page 266

1 ◆ £100

81

On which continent is Great Britain?

- A: Africa
- B: North America
- C: Europe
- D: Australia

82

Which of these words describes a cat
with a brownish-yellow striped coat?

- A: Cabby
- B: Shabby
- C: Tabby
- D: Dabby

83

What name is given to the end part
of a shirt sleeve that covers the wrist?

- A: Ruff
- B: Cuff
- C: Duff
- D: Scuff

84

On which part of the body would 'mittens' be worn?

- A: Hands
- B: Knees
- C: Shoulders
- D: Feet

85

Which of these pairs of words
begins a popular series of jokes?

- A: Rap rap
- B: Tap tap
- C: Knock knock
- D: Bang bang

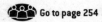
50:50 Go to page 242   Go to page 254   ? Answers on page 266

1 ◆ £100

86

Which of these would you have if you
wanted to make your hands look nice?

A: Manicure

B: Fishicure

C: Birdicure

D: Dogicure

87

How many days are there in a week?

A: One

B: Three

C: Five

D: Seven

88

In which street does the prime minister of Britain live?

page
49

A: Downing Street

B: Upping Street

C: Lefting Street

D: Righting Street

50:50 Go to page 242   Go to page 254   ? Answers on page 266

50:50		
15	**£1 MILLION**	
14	£500,000	
13	£250,000	
12	£125,000	
11	£64,000	
10	**£32,000**	
9	£16,000	
8	£8,000	
7	£4,000	
6	£2,000	
5	**£1,000**	
4	£500	
3	£300	
2	◆	**£200**
1	◆	£100

2 ♦ £200

1

What weapon is traditionally fired from a 'bow'?

- A: Bullet
- B: Arrow
- C: Cannonball
- D: Sword

2

What type of animal is the computer game hero 'Sonic'?

- A: Rabbit
- B: Badger
- C: Ferret
- D: Hedgehog

3

David Beckham represents England at which sport?

- A: Cricket
- B: Golf
- C: Tennis
- D: Football

4

Complete the name of the popular party game: 'Hide-and- ...'?

- A: Discover
- B: Find
- C: Seek
- D: Search

5

Which of these creatures is famous for having fat-filled 'humps' on its back?

- A: Sheep
- B: Camel
- C: Horse
- D: Goat

50:50 Go to page 242   Go to page 254   **?** Answers on page 266

2 ◆ £200

6

In the nursery rhyme, who went
up the hill to fetch a pail of water?

◆A: Hank and Will ◆B: Frank and Bill
◆C: Grant and Phil ◆D: Jack and Jill

7

During which month is an advent
calendar most likely to be used?

◆A: April ◆B: June
◆C: September ◆D: December

8

In the Bible, Noah builds an ark to
escape which natural catastrophe?

◆A: Flood ◆B: Earthquake
◆C: Drought ◆D: Volcanic eruption

page
53

9

Which of these is a soft shoe you would
be most likely to wear around the house?

◆A: Slider ◆B: Skater
◆C: Slipper ◆D: Skidder

10

Which of these is the name of a
long-running children's TV programme?

◆A: Grange Lake ◆B: Grange Mountain
◆C: Grange River ◆D: Grange Hill

50:50 Go to page 242   Go to page 254   ? Answers on page 266

2 ◆ £200

11

Who was the first man to walk on the moon?

- A: Neil Legstrong
- B: Neil Handstrong
- C: Neil Armstrong
- D: Neil Footstrong

12

Where on your body would you normally put a fez or a bowler?

- A: Head
- B: Hand
- C: Foot
- D: Face

13

What type of creature is a vulture?

- A: Snake
- B: Rodent
- C: Bird
- D: Cat

14

Which of these is a flavoured milky drink?

- A: Milkshake
- B: Milkjolt
- C: Milkbump
- D: Milkjerk

15

Porcupines are traditionally covered in what?

- A: Stripes
- B: Spots
- C: Scales
- D: Spines

50:50 Go to page 242   Go to page 254   ? Answers on page 266

2 ◆ £200

16

Which of these is a type of tent historically used by American Indians?

- A: Heepee
- B: Deepee
- C: Teepee
- D: Peepee

17

Which season of the year is particularly associated with leaves falling off trees?

- A: Spring
- B: Summer
- C: Autumn
- D: Winter

18

The tiger is a large variety of which animal?

page 55

- A: Dog
- B: Badger
- C: Rat
- D: Cat

19

Which of these is a vehicle on runners, used for travelling over snow or ice?

- A: Unicycle
- B: Hovercraft
- C: Dinghy
- D: Sledge

20

Which type of travel is associated with Concorde?

- A: Rail
- B: Air
- C: Water
- D: Road

50:50 Go to page 242   Go to page 254   ? Answers on page 266

2 ◆ £200

21

What animals are traditionally kept in an aquarium?

- A: Ducks
- B: Horses
- C: Fish
- D: Cows

22

The bagpipes are a musical instrument traditionally associated with which country?

- A: Scotland
- B: Mexico
- C: China
- D: Argentina

23

Which of these would you use to light a fire?

- A: Match
- B: Tournament
- C: Competition
- D: Game

24

Which of these is an Australian animal?

- A: Elephant
- B: Giraffe
- C: Kangaroo
- D: Rhinoceros

25

What type of food is spaghetti?

- A: Salad
- B: Pasta
- C: Cheese
- D: Bread

50:50 Go to page 242   Go to page 254   ? Answers on page 266

2 ◆ £200

26

Which of these is a host of 'SM: tv Live' with Dec?

A: Fly

B: Bee

C: Bug

D: Ant

27

What type of animal is Rudolph, possessor of a particularly red nose in the title of a song?

A: Rabbit

B: Raven

C: Reindeer

D: Rooster

28

Which of these attracts metal?

A: Magnolia

B: Magnet

C: Magma

D: Magnificat

29

Which item of cutlery traditionally has three prongs?

A: Spoon

B: Knife

C: Fork

D: Ladle

30

What is stuck to a letter to ensure that it reaches its destination?

A: Crunch

B: Thump

C: Stamp

D: Kick

50:50 Go to page 242   Go to page 254   ? Answers on page 266

2 ◆ £200

31

Which of these is a type of Pokémon?

- A: Dongalong
- B: Flobalob
- C: Pikachu
- D: Fubberub

32

Which creatures live in a sty?

- A: Pigs
- B: Cows
- C: Sheep
- D: Goats

33

Grandfather, carriage and cuckoo are types of what?

- A: Spoons
- B: Clocks
- C: Fabric
- D: Umbrellas

34

Which of these animals traditionally has tusks?

- A: Giraffe
- B: Gazelle
- C: Leopard
- D: Elephant

35

Which part of a traditional Christmas dinner is usually stuffed?

- A: Brussels sprouts
- B: Cranberry sauce
- C: Turkey
- D: Plum pudding

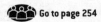 
50:50 Go to page 242   Go to page 254   ? Answers on page 266

2 ◆ £200

36

What term describes the skin of someone who is either frightened or very cold?

- A: Coot flesh
- B: Duck bumps
- C: Goose pimples
- D: Swan hives

37

Which of these do you not associate with rainy weather?

- A: Wellingtons
- B: Mackintosh
- C: Umbrella
- D: Sandals

38

Which of these are regular performers on Children's BBC?

- A: The Giggle Brothers
- B: The Guffaw Brothers
- C: The Belly-laugh Brothers
- D: The Chuckle Brothers

39

Which of these cities is found in Australia?

- A: Stanley
- B: Simon
- C: Sean
- D: Sydney

40

Which member of the Spice Girls married the footballer David Beckham?

- A: Scary Spice
- B: Sporty Spice
- C: Baby Spice
- D: Posh Spice

50:50 Go to page 242   Go to page 254    Answers on page 266

2 ◆ £200

41

Complete this famous cat and mouse
cartoon team: Tom and ...?

- A: Terry
- B: Jerry
- C: Kerry
- D: Cherry

42

Which board game involves removing parts of a
body without making the patient's nose buzz?

- A: Surgery
- B: Operation
- C: Hospital
- D: Doctor

43

Which features of Star Trek's
Mister Spock are famously pointed?

- A: Ears
- B: Hands
- C: Feet
- D: Teeth

44

In the tongue twister, who
'picked a peck of pickled pepper'?

- A: Peregrine Plumber
- B: Patrick Painter
- C: Peter Piper
- D: Percy Printer

45

Which of these is a type of bee?

- A: Jack
- B: King
- C: Queen
- D: Ace

 50:50 Go to page 242　　Go to page 254　　? Answers on page 266

2 ◆ £200

46

Complete the title of the nursery rhyme: 'Mary Had A Little...'?

- A: Lamb
- B: Pig
- C: Cow
- D: Mouse

47

What kind of animal is a poodle?

- A: Cat
- B: Sheep
- C: Dog
- D: Horse

48

Which of these would you find in a computer?

- A: Microchip
- B: Microcrisp
- C: Micronut
- D: Microtwiglet

49

A hiss is a sound most associated with which of these creatures?

- A: Mouse
- B: Sheep
- C: Snake
- D: Dog

50

Which pantomime features a magical lamp?

- A: Cinderella
- B: Aladdin
- C: Sleeping Beauty
- D: Jack and the Beanstalk

50:50 Go to page 242 Go to page 254 **?** Answers on page 266

2 ◆ £200

51

'Belly' is another term for which part of the body?

A: Head   B: Stomach

C: Knee   D: Foot

52

What is said to inhabit Loch Ness in Scotland?

A: Loch Ness Monster   B: Loch Ness Giant

C: Loch Ness Mermaid   D: Loch Ness Fairy

53

Which sport is most associated with Wembley?

A: Hockey   B: Baseball

C: Cricket   D: Football

54

In what type of sum would you see a small line with a dot above and below it?

A: Division   B: Multiplication

C: Addition   D: Subtraction

55

Which of these signs is most likely to be seen on a garden gate?

A: Beware of the hamster   B: Beware of the dog

C: Beware of the armadillo   D: Beware of the children

50:50 Go to page 242   Go to page 254    ? Answers on page 266

2 ◆ £200

56

Which of these creatures has stripes?

- A: Giraffe
- B: Elephant
- C: Zebra
- D: Crocodile

57

Where on your body would you normally wear a plimsoll?

- A: Head
- B: Hand
- C: Foot
- D: Face

58

What does Little Miss Muffet eat in the nursery rhyme?

page
63

- A: Fish and chips
- B: Curds and whey
- C: Bangers and mash
- D: Strawberries and cream

59

Which of these is a popular shape for sugar?

- A: Pyramid
- B: Cube
- C: Cone
- D: Sphere

60

The boomerang is a weapon traditionally associated with which country?

- A: Germany
- B: South Africa
- C: Canada
- D: Australia

50:50 Go to page 242   Go to page 254   ? Answers on page 266

2 ◆ £200

61

Which of these describes something that is convenient and useful to have?

- A: Necky
- B: Army
- C: Handy
- D: Footy

62

Which of these creatures has the most legs?

- A: Tarantula
- B: Hamster
- C: Pigeon
- D: Centipede

63

Which of these is a leading British political party?

- A: Labour Party
- B: Work Party
- C: Graft Party
- D: Toil Party

64

Which part of the body is usually covered by the sleeve of a garment?

- A: Arm
- B: Leg
- C: Foot
- D: Neck

65

Pacific and Atlantic are examples of which geographical feature?

- A: Mountains
- B: Lakes
- C: Oceans
- D: Forests

50:50 Go to page 242   Go to page 254   ? Answers on page 266

2 ◆ £200

66

Which animal would be most likely to sleep in a kennel?

- A: Horse
- B: Chicken
- C: Rabbit
- D: Dog

67

What is the term for a weekday holiday in the UK, such as 1st January?

- A: Post Office Holiday
- B: Building Society Holiday
- C: Supermarket Holiday
- D: Bank Holiday

68

Which of these is another word for an 'eraser'?

page 65

- A: Rubber
- B: Wood
- C: Metal
- D: Plastic

69

On a clock face, which of these indicate the time?

- A: Fingers
- B: Hands
- C: Toes
- D: Feet

70

Which of these sweets is normally sold on a stick?

- A: Gobstopper
- B: Sherbet
- C: Jelly baby
- D: Lollipop

50:50 Go to page 243   Go to page 255   ? Answers on page 266

2 ◆ £200

71

Which of these usually make a house haunted?

- A: Ghosts
- B: Mice
- C: Carol singers
- D: Ants

72

What name is traditionally given to the day after Christmas Day?

- A: Punching Day
- B: Boxing Day
- C: Wrestling Day
- D: Fighting Day

73

The fictional character Tarzan is said to be 'Lord' of which environment?

- A: The sea
- B: The jungle
- C: The skies
- D: The desert

74

What type of food are Cheddar and Stilton?

- A: Cheese
- B: Vegetables
- C: Fruit
- D: Meat

75

Which of these would be used by someone who jumps out of a plane?

- A: Paramour
- B: Parallel
- C: Paradox
- D: Parachute

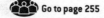
50:50 Go to page 243   Go to page 255   ? Answers on page 266

76

What type of creature is a penguin?

- A: Fish
- B: Bird
- C: Bear
- D: Marsupial

77

Complete the traditional fairy story beginning: 'Once upon a...'?

- A: Dream
- B: Song
- C: Time
- D: Wish

78

Which of these is a general term for a town by the sea where ships can load and unload?

- A: Sherry
- B: Whiskey
- C: Beer
- D: Port

79

In which of these environments would a blue whale live?

- A: In water
- B: In the air
- C: In trees
- D: In space

80

Which of these are tourist attractions in Egypt?

- A: Pyramids
- B: Squares
- C: Circles
- D: Cubes

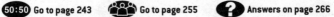

50:50 Go to page 243   Go to page 255   ? Answers on page 266

2 ◆ £200

81

What type of creature is
Winnie-the-Pooh, created by A.A. Milne?

A: Horse
B: Dog
C: Bear
D: Badger

82

Which of these means 'in agreement'?

A: UK
B: DK
C: CK
D: OK

83

What name is given to the young of a lion?

A: Puppy
B: Cub
C: Fledgling
D: Foal

84

Which of these is the title of the wife of a king?

A: Princess
B: Duchess
C: Countess
D: Queen

50:50 Go to page 243   Go to page 255   Answers on page 266

50:50		
15	**£1 MILLION**	
14	£500,000	
13	£250,000	
12	£125,000	
11	£64,000	
10	**£32,000**	
9	£16,000	
8	£8,000	
7	£4,000	
6	£2,000	
5	**£1,000**	
4	£500	
3 ◆	**£300**	
2 ◆	£200	
1 ◆	£100	

3 ◆ £300

1

Which two colours are present
in a 'monochrome' photograph?

A: Blue and red

B: Pink and green

C: Yellow and purple

D: Black and white

2

Which household item can be
found in the word 'chimpanzee'?

A: Bin

B: Cup

C: Tap

D: Pan

3

Fred and his best friend Barney Rubble
are characters in which TV cartoon?

A: Boss Cat

B: The Jetsons

C: Pokémon

D: The Flintstones

4

Which of these is a rodent pet?

A: Guinea cow

B: Guinea horse

C: Guinea goat

D: Guinea pig

5

What is the main ingredient of the dip 'hummus'?

A: Ducklingpeas

B: Chickpeas

C: Kittenpeas

D: Lambpeas

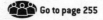 50:50 Go to page 243    Go to page 255   ? Answers on page 266

3 ◆ £300

6

In the Christian religion, the Bible is divided into two testaments, the Old Testament and which other?

- A: Young Testament
- B: Modern Testament
- C: New Testament
- D: Advanced Testament

7

Which bear lives with his friend Boo Boo in Jellystone Park?

- A: Pooh Bear
- B: Paddington Bear
- C: Barney Bear
- D: Yogi Bear

8

Which type of pin has a round head and is particularly used to put notices on walls?

- A: Painting pin
- B: Drawing pin
- C: Writing pin
- D: Scribbling pin

9

Which of these words comes after 'arti' to make a vegetable?

- A: Cough
- B: Choke
- C: Hiccup
- D: Sneeze

10

Which of these is the term for the most important items in a news broadcast?

- A: Noselines
- B: Eyelines
- C: Hairlines
- D: Headlines

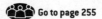 50:50 Go to page 243   Go to page 255    ? Answers on page 266

3 ♦ £300

11

What name is given to a dried grape?

A: Lychee

B: Raisin

C: Kiwi

D: Garlic

12

Which of these left the boy band Take That in 1995?

A: Craig David

B: Robbie Williams

C: Ronan Keating

D: Dane Bowers

13

In which of these sports could you serve an ace?

A: Cricket

B: Tennis

C: Football

D: Hockey

14

What is the name of the screen attached to a computer?

A: Observer

B: Watcher

C: Recorder

D: Monitor

15

Which of these is a type of rotating wind?

A: Torpedo

B: Tomato

C: Tornado

D: Tobacco

50:50 Go to page 243   Go to page 255   ? Answers on page 266

3 ◆ £300

16

Which of these sports is played with an oval ball?

◆ A: Cricket   ◆ B: Snooker

◆ C: Rugby union   ◆ D: Football

17

Which of these words comes after 'performing' and 'martial' to make display activities?

◆ A: Arts   ◆ B: Germans

◆ C: Geographies   ◆ D: Biologies

18

Which of these containers is most likely to be used for a picnic?

page
73

◆ A: Satchel   ◆ B: Hamper

◆ C: Pail   ◆ D: Purse

19

In olden times, who put shoes on horses?

◆ A: Fletcher   ◆ B: Wheeler

◆ C: Blacksmith   ◆ D: Parson

20

In the Bible, how many Commandments did God give to Moses on Mount Sinai?

◆ A: Four   ◆ B: Six

◆ C: Eight   ◆ D: Ten

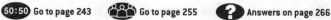

50:50 Go to page 243   Go to page 255   **?** Answers on page 266

3 ◆ £300

21

Which of these marine creatures
has five or more radiating arms?

A: Shark
B: Eel
C: Starfish
D: Stingray

22

What is the total when the numbers of days in the
week are added to the number of months in the year?

A: 14
B: 16
C: 17
D: 19

23

Ken Barlow and Jack Duckworth
live on which famous street?

A: Sesame Street
B: Quality Street
C: Wall Street
D: Coronation Street

24

Which of these would be used to make clay bowls?

A: Baker's wheel
B: Potter's wheel
C: Butcher's wheel
D: Farmer's wheel

25

Which of these is a term for a male chicken?

A: Booster
B: Rooster
C: Hooster
D: Mooster

50:50 Go to page 243   Go to page 255   ? Answers on page 266

3 ◆ £300

page
75

26

Which flower is also the name of a shade of pink?

- A: Rose
- B: Hyacinth
- C: Orchid
- D: Tulip

27

Which of these is a continent?

- A: Africa
- B: Mexico
- C: China
- D: Germany

28

Complete this line from an S Club 7 hit: 'Reach for the...'?

- A: Moon
- B: Stars
- C: Sun
- D: Sky

29

Which of these is a funnel-shaped device for amplifying the voice?

- A: Xylophone
- B: Telephone
- C: Megaphone
- D: Dictaphone

30

Which office would you go to if you wanted to buy tickets for a film or show?

- A: Bag office
- B: Bell office
- C: Bin office
- D: Box office

50:50 Go to page 243   Go to page 255   ? Answers on page 266

3 ◆ £300

31

What is the name of the land featured in the Peter Pan story?

- A: No Way No Way
- B: Not Not
- C: No No
- D: Never Never

32

Which of these abbreviations is most likely to appear at the bottom of an invitation?

- A: RIP
- B: TWA
- C: OHMS
- D: RSVP

33

Which of these cheeses is made backwards?

- A: Cheddar
- B: Double Gloucester
- C: Edam
- D: Brie

34

Which of these would you use to make a cup of 'char'?

- A: Bean bag
- B: Post bag
- C: Kit bag
- D: Tea bag

35

Which of these is a dance?

- A: Tintin
- B: Boxbox
- C: Cancan
- D: Binbin

50:50 Go to page 243   Go to page 255   ? Answers on page 266

3 ◆ £300

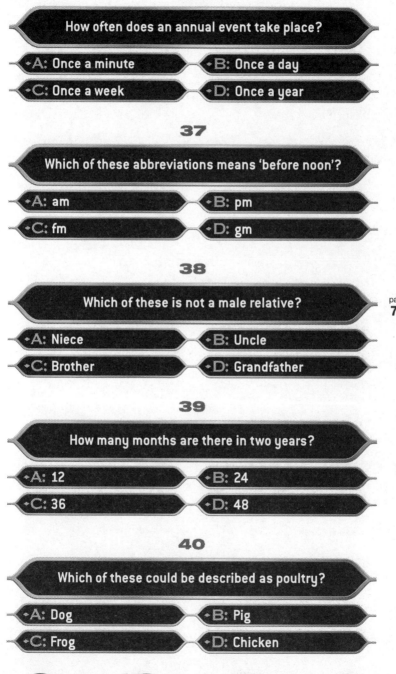

36

How often does an annual event take place?

◆A: Once a minute ◆B: Once a day

◆C: Once a week ◆D: Once a year

37

Which of these abbreviations means 'before noon'?

◆A: am ◆B: pm

◆C: fm ◆D: gm

38

Which of these is not a male relative?

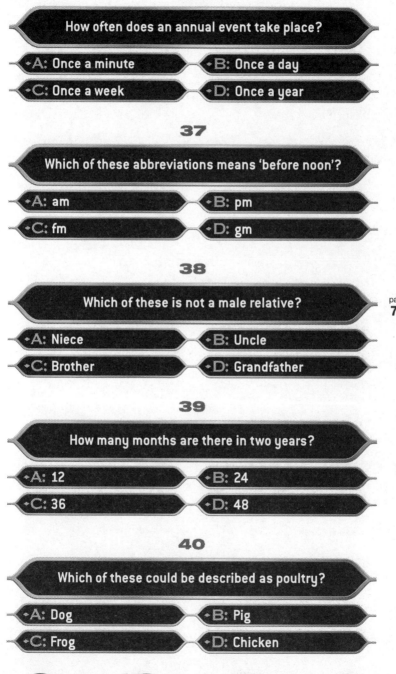

◆A: Niece ◆B: Uncle

◆C: Brother ◆D: Grandfather

39

How many months are there in two years?

◆A: 12 ◆B: 24

◆C: 36 ◆D: 48

40

Which of these could be described as poultry?

◆A: Dog ◆B: Pig

◆C: Frog ◆D: Chicken

50:50 Go to page 243   Go to page 255   ? Answers on page 266

3 ◆ £300

41

Which of these is a synthetic material?

- A: Pegyester
- B: Patyester
- C: Pinyester
- D: Polyester

42

Which nursery rhyme refers to 'all the king's horses'?

- A: Humpty Dumpty
- B: Old Mother Hubbard
- C: Old King Cole
- D: Little Bo Peep

43

Which of these is a species of elephant?

- A: European
- B: African
- C: South American
- D: Australian

44

How many legs are there on an insect?

- A: 4
- B: 6
- C: 8
- D: 10

45

In England, what are the Severn and the Tyne?

- A: Mountains
- B: Rivers
- C: Deserts
- D: Seas

50:50 Go to page 243   Go to page 255   ? Answers on page 266

3 ◆ £300

46

Scarlet is a bright shade of which colour?

- A: White
- B: Black
- C: Red
- D: Blue

47

Which of these is an object kept as a souvenir of a person?

- A: Marengo
- B: Memento
- C: Merino
- D: Morocco

48

Which of these is a musical instrument traditionally made of brass?

- A: Trombone
- B: Guitar
- C: Piano
- D: Violin

49

Which of these is a type of bird of prey?

- A: Falcon
- B: Badger
- C: Trout
- D: Hippo

50

What is the word for something that is added to food to give it more flavour?

- A: Houring
- B: Monthing
- C: Seasoning
- D: Yearing

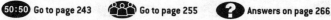 50:50 Go to page 243   Go to page 255   ? Answers on page 266

3 ◆ £300

51

Which of these is not a colour on the Union Jack?

- A: Green
- B: Red
- C: Blue
- D: White

52

Which of these is not a national radio station?

- A: BBC Radio 4
- B: BBC Radio 2
- C: BBC Radio 7
- D: BBC Radio 1

53

**Which item of cutlery would be
most likely to have a serrated edge?**

- A: Teaspoon
- B: Tablespoon
- C: Knife
- D: Fork

54

Which of these letters of the alphabet is not a vowel?

- A: E
- B: O
- C: R
- D: U

55

**Which of these is a small square
chocolate cake with nuts?**

- A: Greenie
- B: Pinkie
- C: Brownie
- D: Creamy

50:50 Go to page 243   Go to page 255   **?** Answers on page 266

3 ◆ £300

56

What name is given to the protective outer layer of trees?

A: Dark | B: Sark
C: Hark | D: Bark

57

Which part of a house may be made from thatch?

A: Roof | B: Chimney
C: Front door | D: Window

58

Which word can come before 'writing', 'cuff' and 'kerchief'?

page 81

A: Bell | B: Hand
C: Band | D: Half

59

On which part of the human body is the palm?

A: Foot | B: Head
C: Leg | D: Hand

60

Which of these is not a traffic light colour?

A: Red | B: Amber
C: Green | D: Blue

50:50 Go to page 243   Go to page 255   ? Answers on page 266

3 ◆ £300

61

Which of these is a breed of dog?

- A: Wrestler
- B: Skater
- C: Boxer
- D: Runner

62

Which of these is a sheet of glass in a window?

- A: Pane
- B: Ake
- C: Kramp
- D: Hert

63

Who was the arch-enemy of the magical Peter Pan?

- A: Captain Nemo
- B: Captain Hook
- C: Captain Ahab
- D: Captain Bligh

64

Complete the title of the Andrew Lloyd Webber musical: 'Starlight...'?

- A: Express
- B: Mail
- C: Sun
- D: Telegraph

65

Which of these is a wart on the foot?

- A: Veronica
- B: Vanessa
- C: Verruca
- D: Valery

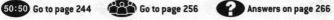 **50:50** Go to page 244   Go to page 256   **?** Answers on page 266

3 ◆ £300

66

Which of these animals grows antlers on its head?

A: Dog

B: Horse

C: Pig

D: Deer

67

Which of these people would be most likely to regularly make use of an x-ray machine?

A: Doctor

B: Vicar

C: Pilot

D: Fisherman

68

In which sport can people score a 'hole-in-one'?

A: Cricket

B: Football

C: Golf

D: Hockey

69

Which of these is a group of characters created by Enid Blyton?

A: Famous Five

B: Super Seven

C: Tremendous Two

D: Wonderful One

70

Oars are used to propel what kind of vehicle?

A: Car

B: Bicycle

C: Boat

D: Glider

50:50 Go to page 244   Go to page 256   ? Answers on page 266

3 ◆ £300

71

Which of these is part of the leg of a cooked chicken?

- A: Violin bow
- B: Oboe reed
- C: Trumpet valve
- D: Drumstick

72

Which of these is a popular science fiction TV programme?

- A: The W-Files
- B: The X-Files
- C: The Y-Files
- D: The Z-Files

73

Which of these would you use to heat up your meal?

- A: Microscope
- B: Microwave
- C: Microphone
- D: Microprocessor

74

What type of creature is the cartoon character Scooby Doo?

- A: Cat
- B: Horse
- C: Dog
- D: Hamster

75

Which of these would you need if your car battery goes flat?

- A: Jump-start
- B: Up-start
- C: Leap-start
- D: Jam-start

page 84

50:50 Go to page 244　　👥 Go to page 256　　❓ Answers on page 266

3 ◆ £300

76

What number comes after 999?

- A: One thousand
- B: One million
- C: One billion
- D: One zillion

77

Which of these animals has a 'bill'?

- A: Goose
- B: Monkey
- C: Horse
- D: Donkey

78

On which part of the body would a contact lens usually be worn?

page 85

- A: Toe
- B: Ear
- C: Eye
- D: Hip

79

In which of these sports are competitors required to wear gloves?

- A: Swimming
- B: Boxing
- C: Snooker
- D: Tennis

80

Which of these animals is known for its bushy tail and fondness for nuts?

- A: Squirrel
- B: Badger
- C: Mole
- D: Dormouse

 50:50 Go to page 244   Go to page 256   Answers on page 266

50:50	☎	👥👥

15	**£1 MILLION**
14	£500,000
13	£250,000
12	£125,000
11	£64,000
10	**£32,000**
9	£16,000
8	£8,000
7	£4,000
6	£2,000
5	**£1,000**
4 ◆	**£500**
3 ◆	£300
2 ◆	£200
1 ◆	£100

4 ◆ £500

1

What is the traditional mode of transport for witches?

A: Hoover

B: Broomstick

C: Feather duster

D: Dustpan and brush

2

Which of these is someone who chooses to live totally alone?

A: Hismit

B: Hermit

C: Yourmit

D: Ourmit

3

Complete the phrase meaning clean and tidy: 'Spick and...'?

A: Spud

B: Spot

C: Span

D: Sped

4

Which of these is a type of board game?

A: Snakes and Ladders

B: Lizards and Ropes

C: Insects and Slides

D: Rats and Drainpipes

5

Which of these is a computer-generated form of communication?

A: B-mail

B: C-mail

C: D-mail

D: E-mail

50:50 Go to page 244   Go to page 256   ? Answers on page 267

4 ◆ £500

6

What type of creature is Walt Disney's 'Bambi'?

A: Deer
B: Horse
C: Cow
D: Dog

7

Which of these legendary characters released a wish-granting genie?

A: Aladdin
B: Hercules
C: King Arthur
D: Pocahontas

8

Which of these creatures is most likely to have prickles?

A: Hedgehog
B: Mole
C: Weasel
D: Squirrel

9

What is the term for a number of young born to an animal at one time?

A: Rubbish
B: Garbage
C: Litter
D: Debris

10

Which of these could be used to play computer games?

A: Funrod
B: Laughpole
C: Happypost
D: Joystick

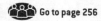 50:50 Go to page 244   Go to page 256   ? Answers on page 267

4 ◆ £500

11

Lara Croft is the heroine of
which popular computer game?

- A: Tomb Raider
- B: Crypt Hunter
- C: Grave Robber
- D: Mausoleum Snatcher

12

In which famous story does a young girl visit
her grandmother and encounter a wolf?

- A: Hansel and Gretel
- B: The Frog Princess
- C: Little Red Riding-Hood
- D: The Ugly Duckling

13

Which of these is a famous frog?

- A: Sooty
- B: Paddington
- C: Kermit
- D: Elmo

14

In Enid Blyton's books, who is
the best friend of Big Ears?

- A: Noddy
- B: Boddy
- C: Coddy
- D: Doddy

15

Which of these is the term for the space under the roof?

- A: Basement
- B: Cellar
- C: Bunker
- D: Loft

 50:50 Go to page 244   Go to page 256   ? Answers on page 267

4 ◆ £500

16

In folklore, what creatures did the
Pied Piper lead out of the town of Hamelin?

◆A: Snakes ◆B: Spiders

◆C: Rats ◆D: Beetles

17

Which of these is a fictional bear
created by Michael Bond?

◆A: Euston ◆B: King's Cross

◆C: Paddington ◆D: Charing Cross

18

In the famous puppet show, who is the wife of Mr Punch?

page
91

◆A: Julie ◆B: Janie

◆C: Jilly ◆D: Judy

19

In the works of Lewis Carroll,
who had 'Adventures in Wonderland'?

◆A: Alexandra ◆B: Alice

◆C: Alison ◆D: Anne

20

What is the name of the mischievous Gaul in a
series of cartoon books by Goscinny and Uderzo?

◆A: Tintin ◆B: Lucky Luke

◆C: Asterix ◆D: Captain Haddock

50:50 Go to page 244   Go to page 256   ? Answers on page 267

4 ◆ £500

21

Which fictional creatures live under Wimbledon Common?

A: Wombles

B: Hobbits

C: Borrowers

D: Teletubbies

22

Anakin Skywalker and Jar Jar Binks are characters in which science fiction film?

A: The Matrix

B: Mouse Hunt

C: The Phantom Menace

D: Stuart Little

23

Which of these creatures begins life as a tadpole?

A: Toad

B: Snake

C: Butterfly

D: Spider

24

Who co-hosts 'SM:TV Live' on Saturday mornings?

A: Cat Deeley

B: Lamb Deeley

C: Horse Deeley

D: Mouse Deeley

25

Which of these does not mean a flow of liquid in a slow thin stream?

A: Trickle

B: Gush

C: Ooze

D: Dribble

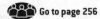
50:50 Go to page 244   Go to page 256   ? Answers on page 267

4 ◆ £500

26

Which of these foods does not have a sweet taste?

A: Honey

B: Treacle

C: Golden syrup

D: Vinegar

27

Which of these is not one of the girls in S Club 7?

A: Tina

B: Katy

C: Hannah

D: Jo

28

The flamingo bird is usually which colour?

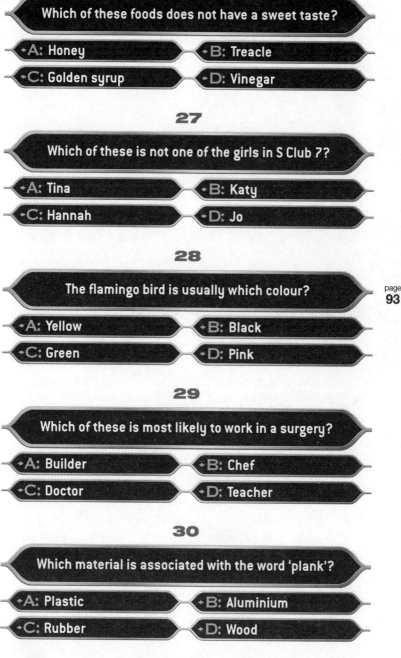

A: Yellow

B: Black

C: Green

D: Pink

29

Which of these is most likely to work in a surgery?

A: Builder

B: Chef

C: Doctor

D: Teacher

30

Which material is associated with the word 'plank'?

A: Plastic

B: Aluminium

C: Rubber

D: Wood

50:50 Go to page 244   Go to page 256   ? Answers on page 267

4 ◆ £500

31

Which of these is the name of an ancient stone circle in Wiltshire?

◆A: Bonehenge   ◆B: Stonehenge

◆C: Conehenge   ◆D: Domehenge

32

Which girl's name is also a decorative Christmas plant?

◆A: Holly   ◆B: Polly

◆C: Molly   ◆D: Dolly

33

Someone in good health could be said to be 'alive and...' what?

◆A: Punching   ◆B: Kicking

◆C: Screaming   ◆D: Slapping

34

Which of these is a theme park in Staffordshire?

◆A: Alton Turrets   ◆B: Alton Tunnels

◆C: Alton Temples   ◆D: Alton Towers

35

Which of these is a practice run of the things you should do in the event of a fire?

◆A: Fire saw   ◆B: Fire plane

◆C: Fire drill   ◆D: Fire lathe

50:50 Go to page 244   Go to page 256   Answers on page 267

4 ♦ £500

36

'Bill' is usually a shortened version of which name?

- A: Dillon
- B: William
- C: Miles
- D: Philip

37

Which of these animals builds dams and lives in a lodge?

- A: Beaver
- B: Bear
- C: Bison
- D: Badger

38

In which racket sport do the players hit a shuttlecock?

- A: Lawn tennis
- B: Squash
- C: Badminton
- D: Real tennis

39

Which of these is an informal word for 'father'?

- A: Whip
- B: Snap
- C: Crackle
- D: Pop

40

What mode of transportation is a gondola?

- A: Car
- B: Boat
- C: Bicycle
- D: Hovercraft

50:50 Go to page 244   Go to page 256   Answers on page 267

4 ◆ £500

41

Which day only occurs once every four years?

- A: 31st April
- B: 31st June
- C: 30th September
- D: 29th February

42

By what name is the harmonica also known?

- A: Foot organ
- B: Heel organ
- C: Mouth organ
- D: Knee organ

43

What animals are traditionally kept in a hive?

- A: Horses
- B: Bees
- C: Sheep
- D: Dogs

44

Which name is shared by two of the Spice Girls?

- A: Victoria
- B: Emma
- C: Melanie
- D: Geri

45

Which creatures feature in the film 'Jurassic Park'?

- A: Wolves
- B: Dinosaurs
- C: Sharks
- D: Snakes

50:50 Go to page 244   Go to page 256   ? Answers on page 267

4 ◆ £500

46

Complete the title of this C.S. Lewis book: 'The Lion, the Witch and the...'?

A: Wardrobe

B: Tallboy

C: Dresser

D: Cupboard

47

Which of these people is particularly associated with 5th November?

A: Guy Fawkes

B: Robin Hood

C: Dick Turpin

D: Sweeney Todd

48

In which part of a scorpion's body is its sting?

A: Front legs

B: Mouth

C: Nose

D: Tail

49

Which of these is a member of Steps?

A: Faye

B: Kaye

C: Gaye

D: Maye

50

What is the 'toad' in the dish 'toad-in-the-hole'?

A: Sausage

B: Bacon

C: Meatball

D: Faggot

50:50 Go to page 244 Go to page 256 ? Answers on page 267

4 ◆ £500

51

Which British king used the magical sword Excalibur?

- A: Arthur
- B: Henry VIII
- C: Richard the Lionheart
- D: William the Conqueror

52

According to the proverb, 'A stitch in time saves...' how many?

- A: Three
- B: Five
- C: Seven
- D: Nine

53

Which classic 1939 film features the Tin Man, Scarecrow and Dorothy?

- A: The Witches of Eastwick
- B: The Wizard of Oz
- C: The Sorcerer's Apprentice
- D: The Magician's House

54

How many days are there in the month of May?

- A: 28
- B: 29
- C: 30
- D: 31

55

Which of these occupations is most associated with Popeye?

- A: Tinker
- B: Tailor
- C: Soldier
- D: Sailor

 50:50 Go to page 244   Go to page 256   ? Answers on page 267

4 ♦ £500

56

Pizza is a dish originating in which country?

A: Switzerland
B: Italy
C: Germany
D: France

57

Which of these fairy tale characters is the smallest?

A: Cinderella
B: Tom Thumb
C: Snow White
D: Sleeping Beauty

58

Which of these is a name for someone
who takes part in a competition?

A: Contestant
B: Consultant
C: Congregant
D: Consignment

59

Which of these women was an ancient queen of Egypt?

A: Margaret Thatcher
B: Madonna
C: Cleopatra
D: Donna Air

60

What is measured on the Fahrenheit scale?

A: Wind force
B: Temperature
C: Water pollution
D: Acidity

 50:50 Go to page 245   Go to page 257   ? Answers on page 267

4 ◆ £500

61

Which of these is the title of a 1994 animated Disney film?

◆A: The Tiger Prince ◆B: The Panther Queen

◆C: The Leopard Princess ◆D: The Lion King

62

Who assists the bridegroom at a wedding?

◆A: Good man ◆B: Well man

◆C: Better man ◆D: Best man

63

Which of these sports uses a bat?

◆A: Volleyball ◆B: Basketball

◆C: Baseball ◆D: Badminton

64

Which pantomime character has two ugly sisters?

◆A: Sleeping Beauty ◆B: Aladdin

◆C: Cinderella ◆D: Snow White

65

What type of creature was the mythical phoenix?

◆A: Bird ◆B: Bear

◆C: Horse ◆D: Dog

50:50 Go to page 245   Go to page 257   ? Answers on page 267

4 ◆ £500

66

Which of these is a suit in a standard pack of cards?

- A: Livers
- B: Kidneys
- C: Spleens
- D: Hearts

67

Charles was the first name of which author?

- A: Dickens
- B: Barrie
- C: Milne
- D: Travers

68

Which of these is a word to describe a large building?

page **101**

- A: Horizonhugger
- B: Skyscraper
- C: Heavenscratcher
- D: Roofreacher

69

The Riddler and the Joker are the enemies of which hero?

- A: Spiderman
- B: Action Man
- C: Batman
- D: Bananaman

70

Which of these creatures has gills to breathe through?

- A: Hamster
- B: Parrot
- C: Cat
- D: Goldfish

 **50:50** Go to page 245   Go to page 257   **?** Answers on page 267

4 ◆ £500

71

If something is drenched, it is extremely what?

A: Hot | B: Bitter
C: Wet | D: Sharp

72

Which of these men was famous
for composing classical music?

A: Bach | B: Einstein
C: Columbus | D: Pepys

73

Which of these is a woollen hood that covers your
head and neck, leaving just your face exposed?

A: Anorak | B: Balaclava
C: Cummerbund | D: Dungaree

74

Which of these is most likely to say 'Hocus Pocus'?

A: Conjuror | B: Line dancer
C: Film director | D: Racing commentator

75

What does the letter 'R' stand for
in the school lesson R.E.?

A: Regimental | B: Recreational
C: Religious | D: Revolutionary

50:50 Go to page 245   Go to page 257   Answers on page 267

Which country is famous for its haggis?

A: Germany | B: Scotland

C: Italy | D: Spain

50:50 Go to page 245   Go to page 257   Answers on page 267

50:50		

15 **£1 MILLION**

14 £500,000

13 £250,000

12 £125,000

11 £64,000

10 **£32,000**

9 £16,000

8 £8,000

7 £4,000

6 £2,000

5 ◆ £1,000

4 ◆ £500

3 ◆ £300

2 ◆ £200

1 ◆ £100

5 ◆ £1,000

1

Paul McCartney and John Lennon
were members of which pop group?

- A: Beatles
- B: Spyders
- C: Cokroaches
- D: Flies

2

What is the unit of currency in France?

- A: Frederic
- B: Franc
- C: Finn
- D: Flavio

3

Steven Spielberg is a famous what?

- A: Film director
- B: Fashion designer
- C: Food manufacturer
- D: Footballer

4

Which of these is a glass lens worn
to improve the sight in one eye?

- A: Monopoly
- B: Monocle
- C: Monorail
- D: Monolith

5

Which of these is a long steady ride
through the countryside on a horse?

- A: Hack
- B: Nack
- C: Jack
- D: Lack

50:50 Go to page 245   Go to page 257   ? Answers on page 267

5 ◆ £1,000

6

Mick Jagger is the lead singer in which rock group?

- A: Tumbling Boulders
- B: Rolling Stones
- C: Falling Pebbles
- D: Sliding Rocks

7

What is the total when a century is added to half a dozen?

- A: 32
- B: 54
- C: 106
- D: 118

8

Tim Henman is a leading figure in which of these sports?

- A: Cricket
- B: Football
- C: Tennis
- D: Rugby

9

Which of these does not mean to have something on a temporary basis?

- A: Borrow
- B: Hire
- C: Purchase
- D: Loan

10

Which fictional character is known as 'the boy who wouldn't grow up'?

- A: Peter Pan
- B: Bilbo Baggins
- C: Huckleberry Finn
- D: Harry Potter

50:50 Go to page 245   Go to page 257   Answers on page 267

5 ◆ £1,000

11

What is the name of the river that flows through London?

◆A: Severn ◆B: Avon

◆C: Dee ◆D: Thames

12

Which animal-loving doctor has been played by Eddie Murphy in two recent films?

◆A: Doctor Zhivago ◆B: Doctor Kildare

◆C: Doctor Dolittle ◆D: Doctor Quinn

13

Proverbially, what are you said to have on your face if you look foolish?

◆A: Egg ◆B: Bacon

◆C: Sausage ◆D: Beans

14

Which of the five senses would you associate with the word 'aroma'?

◆A: Smell ◆B: Sight

◆C: Hearing ◆D: Touch

15

What is a hoedown?

◆A: Farming tool ◆B: Waterproof coat

◆C: Mushroom ◆D: Square dance

50:50 Go to page 245 Go to page 257 **?** Answers on page 267

5 ◆ £1,000

16

Who played James Bond in the film 'The World Is Not Enough'?

A: Leonardo DiCaprio
B: Brad Pitt
C: Jim Carrey
D: Pierce Brosnan

17

In the popular cartoons, who is Wile E. Coyote constantly chasing?

A: Daffy Duck
B: Mickey Mouse
C: Popeye
D: Roadrunner

18

Thailand is a country on which continent?

page
109

A: Africa
B: Europe
C: North America
D: Asia

19

Dublin is a city in which European country?

A: Ireland
B: France
C: Germany
D: Denmark

20

'Swine' is another name for which farmyard animal?

A: Horse
B: Sheep
C: Pig
D: Cow

50:50 Go to page 245   Go to page 257   ❓ Answers on page 267

5 ◆ £1,000

21

Which of these is a state of Australia?

A: New South Scotland

B: New South England

C: New South Wales

D: New South Ireland

22

In which game do contestants aim for the 'jack'?

A: Snooker

B: Darts

C: Bowls

D: Tennis

23

Which of these items could be a 'four-poster'?

A: Bed

B: Bath

C: Oven

D: Toilet

24

Complete the title of the Dr Seuss book: 'Green Eggs and...'?

A: Chips

B: Ham

C: Sausages

D: Chickens

25

Katy Hill and Konnie Huq have both presented which children's TV show?

A: Blue Peter

B: Record Breakers

C: How 2

D: Newsround

50:50 Go to page 245   Go to page 257   ? Answers on page 267

5 ♦ £1,000

26

Which of these creatures is most likely to have pincers?

A: Kangaroo

B: Reindeer

C: Lobster

D: Rat

27

From which language does the phrase 'déjà vu' come?

A: Greek

B: French

C: Norwegian

D: Welsh

28

What type of life form are mushrooms and toadstools?

A: Jealousgi

B: Tallgi

C: Fungi

D: Sadgi

29

Which of these is not an anagram of the word 'post'?

A: Stop

B: Pots

C: Sport

D: Spot

30

Who was the famous dancing partner of Fred Astaire?

A: Baby Rogers

B: Sporty Rogers

C: Ginger Rogers

D: Posh Rogers

50:50 Go to page 245   Go to page 257   Answers on page 267

5 ◆ £1,000

31

'Vixen' is a name given to the female of which animal?

- A: Cow
- B: Fox
- C: Bear
- D: Horse

32

Which of these is the correct spelling?

- A: Adress
- B: Addres
- C: Adres
- D: Address

33

How many members are there in the pop group A1?

- A: Three
- B: Four
- C: Five
- D: Six

34

What is usually stored in a larder?

- A: Clothes
- B: Food
- C: Cars
- D: Hay

35

Which of these means wanting something very much?

- A: Talling
- B: Longing
- C: Larging
- D: Bigging

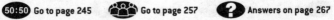 50:50 Go to page 245   Go to page 257   ? Answers on page 267

5 ♦ £1,000

36

Which book is used to keep a record of a journey by boat?

- A: Twigbook
- B: Stickbook
- C: Branchbook
- D: Logbook

37

Which valuable item is often found in oysters?

- A: Diamond
- B: Ruby
- C: Pearl
- D: Emerald

38

Which of these musical instruments is played in an upright position between the player's knees?

page
113

- A: Violin
- B: Cello
- C: Guitar
- D: Viola

39

What is the 17th letter of the alphabet?

- A: M
- B: O
- C: Q
- D: R

40

What is the official currency of Spain?

- A: Franc
- B: Dollar
- C: Mark
- D: Peseta

50:50 Go to page 245   Go to page 257   ? Answers on page 267

5 ◆ £1,000

41

Which of these cheeses is usually sold
with a red waxy coating around the edge?

- A: Cheddar
- B: Brie
- C: Edam
- D: Red Leicester

42

Which of these is a type of fish?

- A: Snorkel
- B: Skate
- C: Skittle
- D: Ski

43

Michael Jordan was a major star in which sport?

- A: Football
- B: Basketball
- C: Cricket
- D: Tennis

44

Which word describes the letters of
the alphabet that are not vowels?

- A: Constellations
- B: Constants
- C: Continents
- D: Consonants

45

Which of these is not a dinosaur?

- A: Tyrannosaurus
- B: Brachiosaurus
- C: Stegosaurus
- D: Thesaurus

50:50 Go to page 245   Go to page 257   ? Answers on page 267

5 ◆ £1,000

46

Which abbreviation indicates that you should look on the other side of a sheet of paper?

- A: PLO
- B: PTO
- C: PG
- D: POV

47

What name is given to a male duck?

- A: Cygnet
- B: Drake
- C: Gosling
- D: Cob

48

Which of these is Pauline Fowler's son in 'EastEnders'?

- A: Matthew
- B: Mark
- C: Luke
- D: John

49

Who was on the throne at the time of the Spanish Armada?

- A: Elizabeth I
- B: Mary I
- C: Anne
- D: Victoria

50

Which fruit shares its name with the girlfriend of the cartoon character Popeye?

- A: Peach
- B: Plum
- C: Olive
- D: Orange

50:50 Go to page 245   Go to page 257   **?** Answers on page 267

5 ◆ £1,000

51

Which of these was a classical composer?

- A: Isaac Newton
- B: Johann Strauss
- C: Pablo Picasso
- D: Rudolf Nureyev

52

Which of these birds shares its name with a chesspiece?

- A: Magpie
- B: Raven
- C: Rook
- D: Pigeon

53

What type of creature is Baloo in 'The Jungle Book'?

- A: Bear
- B: Snake
- C: Ape
- D: Panther

54

For which of these sports do competitors 'weigh in'?

- A: Badminton
- B: Basketball
- C: Boxing
- D: Bowls

55

Which of these vegetables is said to be particularly good for the eyesight?

- A: Cabbage
- B: Cauliflower
- C: Courgette
- D: Carrot

50:50 Go to page 245   Go to page 257   ? Answers on page 267

5 ◆ £1,000

56

Which game has pawns and castles?

- A: Draughts
- B: Snakes and ladders
- C: Monopoly
- D: Chess

57

Which of these is not a gemstone?

- A: Jade
- B: Ruby
- C: Pearl
- D: Gladys

58

What is the capital of Scotland?

- A: Dublin
- B: Cardiff
- C: Edinburgh
- D: London

59

How many years are there in a decade and a half?

- A: 5
- B: 10
- C: 15
- D: 20

60

Which of these is a type of hard, brittle toffee?

- A: Jamscotch
- B: Honeyscotch
- C: Butterscotch
- D: Marmaladescotch

50:50 Go to page 245   Go to page 258   **?** Answers on page 267

5 ♦ £1,000

61

The piccolo is a smaller version of which musical instrument?

- A: Trombone
- B: Double bass
- C: Flute
- D: Guitar

62

Who are the Flowerpot Men?

- A: Brian and Bertie
- B: Bill and Ben
- C: Barry and Bertram
- D: Bob and Bernard

63

What type of weapon was the American Indian tomahawk?

- A: Arrow
- B: Mace
- C: Axe
- D: Hammer

64

Alan Titchmarsh is an expert in which field?

- A: Wines
- B: Football
- C: Gardening
- D: Cooking

65

The cheetah belongs to which family of animals?

- A: Dog
- B: Cat
- C: Bear
- D: Horse

50:50 Go to page 246   Go to page 258   ? Answers on page 267

5 ◆ £1,000

66

What is the official currency of Italy?

◆A: Dollar
◆B: Yen
◆C: Shilling
◆D: Lira

67

Ringo Starr was the drummer for which pop group?

◆A: The Beatles
◆B: Oasis
◆C: Five
◆D: Steps

68

On which part of your body would you wear a beret?

page
119

◆A: Hands
◆B: Feet
◆C: Legs
◆D: Head

69

**Which marine creature can stun
its prey with an electrical charge?**

◆A: Electric shark
◆B: Electric eel
◆C: Electric jellyfish
◆D: Electric starfish

70

**Aerosol gases harm which layer
of the Earth's atmosphere?**

◆A: Bozone
◆B: Crowzone
◆C: Hozone
◆D: Ozone

50:50 Go to page 246   Go to page 258   ? Answers on page 267

5 ◆ £1,000

71

What was the first name of the
comedian Laurel, partner of Hardy?

A: Sid

B: Stan

C: Sam

D: Sven

72

Which of these birds cannot fly?

A: Eagle

B: Thrush

C: Blackbird

D: Kiwi

 50:50 Go to page 246   Go to page 258    ? Answers on page 267

| 50:50 | | |

15   **£1 MILLION**

14   £500,000

13   £250,000

12   £125,000

11   £64,000

10   **£32,000**

9   £16,000

8   £8,000

7   £4,000

6 ◆ £2,000

5 ◆ £1,000

4 ◆ £500

3 ◆ £300

2 ◆ £200

1 ◆ £100

6 ◆ £2,000

1

What type of creature is the film star 'Lassie'?

A: Horse
B: Dog
C: Monkey
D: Dolphin

2

On a standard keyboard, which key is pressed to make all the letters type in upper case?

A: Tab
B: Caps Lock
C: Alt
D: Control

3

Which of these was a notorious outlaw of the American Wild West?

A: Ned Kelly
B: Dick Turpin
C: Ronnie Biggs
D: Billy the Kid

4

Bilbo Baggins is a character in which of these books?

A: The Hobbit
B: The Borrowers
C: Gulliver's Travels
D: The B.F.G.

5

Which of these phrases means to waste time by being slow?

A: Bolly-billy
B: Rally-rully
C: Telly-tolly
D: Dilly-dally

50:50 Go to page 246   Go to page 258   ? Answers on page 267

6 ◆ £2,000

6

Which of these creatures does the hyena most resemble?

- A: Giraffe
- B: Camel
- C: Dog
- D: Crocodile

7

In the Harry Potter books, what is the first name of Harry's friend Miss Granger?

- A: Hermione
- B: Hepzibah
- C: Hannah
- D: Helen

8

Complete the proverb: 'If you can't beat 'em...'?

- A: Leave 'em
- B: Fight 'em
- C: Join 'em
- D: Eat 'em

9

In which American city is the Golden Gate Bridge?

- A: San Francisco
- B: Las Vegas
- C: Boston
- D: New York

10

James T. Kirk and Scotty are characters in which science fiction series?

- A: Lost In Space
- B: Stargate SG-1
- C: Doctor Who
- D: Star Trek

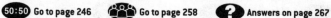

50:50 Go to page 246   Go to page 258   ? Answers on page 267

6 ◆ £2,000

11

What does an eavesdropper specifically do?

- **A: Listens to conversations**
- **B: Tells fibs**
- **C: Breaks promises**
- **D: Tells jokes**

12

Which of these is a group of stars in our galaxy?

- **A: Snowy Way**
- **B: Creamy Way**
- **C: Milky Way**
- **D: Icy Way**

13

What would you normally do with a 'flapjack'?

- **A: Eat it**
- **B: Wear it**
- **C: Put it on a horse**
- **D: Keep it in a cage**

14

The Eiffel Tower is a tourist attraction in which city?

- **A: London**
- **B: Paris**
- **C: Berlin**
- **D: Madrid**

15

Traditionally, how many Wonders of the Ancient World were there?

- **A: 7**
- **B: 17**
- **C: 70**
- **D: 700**

50:50 Go to page 246   Go to page 258   ? Answers on page 267

6 ◆ £2,000

16

Luke Skywalker is a character
in which science fiction film?

- A: The Matrix
- B: Star Wars
- C: Alien
- D: The Terminator

17

Which prehistoric animal was a type of large elephant?

- A: Mammoth
- B: Triceratops
- C: Velociraptor
- D: Tyrannosaurus

18

In what type of house does Jim Henson's TV 'Bear' live?

- A: Big Blue House
- B: Large Red House
- C: Enormous Orange House
- D: Giant Green House

19

Which of these sporting events takes
place once every four years?

- A: FA Cup Final
- B: Grand National
- C: Olympic Games
- D: Superbowl

20

Which of these is the name of a popular toy
and a character in the film 'Toy Story'?

- A: Mr Carrot Head
- B: Mr Swede Head
- C: Mr Spinach Head
- D: Mr Potato Head

 50:50 Go to page 246   Go to page 258   ? Answers on page 267

6 ◆ £2,000

21

Which of these is the title of a Shakespeare play?

A: Romeo and Joyce

B: Romeo and Jennifer

C: Romeo and Julianne

D: Romeo and Juliet

22

The river Nile flows through which of these countries?

A: South Africa

B: Egypt

C: Turkey

D: France

23

Which of these is an informal term for a very sad film?

A: Tear-tipper

B: Tear-burster

C: Tear-jerker

D: Tear-pointer

24

In 'The Muppet Christmas Carol', who plays Ebenezer Scrooge?

A: John Cleese

B: Michael Caine

C: Kermit the Frog

D: Fozzie Bear

25

Which of these units of weight is the heaviest?

A: Pound

B: Ounce

C: Stone

D: Ton

50:50 Go to page 246   Go to page 258   ? Answers on page 267

6 ◆ £2,000

26

Julius Caesar was the ruler of which ancient empire?

◆A: Egyptian ◆B: Ottoman

◆C: Roman ◆D: British

27

Which of these is a famous WWF wrestler?

◆A: The Rock ◆B: The Boulder

◆C: The Pebble ◆D: The Gravel

28

**Clark Kent is the secret identity
of which comic strip superhero?**

◆A: Superman ◆B: Batman

◆C: Green Lantern ◆D: The Flash

29

Which of these means trendy and up-to-date?

◆A: Knee ◆B: Hip

◆C: Wrist ◆D: Toe

30

**Something 'oriental' would come
from which of these countries?**

◆A: Ireland ◆B: Canada

◆C: Greece ◆D: China

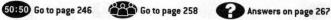 **50:50** Go to page 246 **Go to page 258** **?** Answers on page 267

6 ◆ £2,000

31

'Genie in a Bottle' was a number one hit single for which pop singer?

- A: Britney Spears
- B: Billie Piper
- C: Christina Aguilera
- D: Lolly

32

What is the name for the wax structure bees make to store honey?

- A: Honeybrush
- B: Honeycomb
- C: Honeymirror
- D: Honeyscissors

33

Who had a number one hit single with 'Can We Fix It'?

- A: Bob the Builder
- B: Postman Pat
- C: Fireman Sam
- D: Bertha

34

What was the name of Thomas the Tank Engine's boss?

- A: The Chubby Commandant
- B: The Portly Commodore
- C: The Stout Captain
- D: The Fat Controller

35

What type of food would you be eating if you were served a poppadom as an accompaniment?

- A: Chinese
- B: Italian
- C: Indian
- D: French

 50:50 Go to page 246   Go to page 258   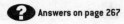 ? Answers on page 267

6 ◆ £2,000

36

The Cheshire Cat is a character in which book?

A: The Hobbit

B: Robinson Crusoe

C: Alice's Adventures in Wonderland

D: Stig of the Dump

37

Which vegetable gave Popeye his amazing strength?

A: Turnip

B: Potato

C: Spinach

D: Marrow

38

Which of these words does not suggest a large amount of money?

A: Pittance

B: Fortune

C: Wealth

D: Opulence

39

Donatello and Michelangelo are teenage mutant ninja varieties of which animal?

A: Tortoise

B: Turtle

C: Terrapin

D: Tarantula

40

The Statue of Liberty is a tourist attraction in the harbour of which city?

A: Chicago

B: New York

C: Los Angeles

D: Miami

 50:50 Go to page 246   Go to page 258   Answers on page 267

6 ◆ £2,000

41

Jason Orange was a member of which boy band?

A: Boyzone
B: Take That
C: Brother Beyond
D: Five

42

Somalia is a country in which continent?

A: South America
B: Asia
C: Africa
D: Europe

43

Complete the name of this famous cartoon strip character: Charlie ...?

A: Black
B: Green
C: Grey
D: Brown

44

To which section of an orchestra does the clarinet belong?

A: Percussion
B: Woodwind
C: Brass
D: Strings

45

What is the name of the island featured in the TV series 'Thunderbirds'?

A: Tracy
B: Sharon
C: Melinda
D: Natalie

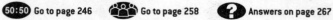

50:50 Go to page 246   Go to page 258   Answers on page 267

6 ◆ £2,000

46

The phrase 'World Wide Web' is most associated with which modern invention?

- A: Internet
- B: Interbox
- C: Intersack
- D: Interbag

47

What type of creatures are the 'Blue Peter' pets Kari and Oke?

- A: Tortoises
- B: Horses
- C: Dogs
- D: Cats

48

In which county is Land's End?

- A: Kent
- B: Norfolk
- C: Cornwall
- D: Lancashire

49

Derived from the French for 'wine', what is the term for an area where grapes are grown?

- A: Nursery
- B: Vineyard
- C: Orchard
- D: Plantation

50

What type of creature is the cartoon character Speedy Gonzales?

- A: Ostrich
- B: Mouse
- C: Bear
- D: Turtle

50:50 Go to page 246   Go to page 258   ? Answers on page 267

6 ◆ £2,000

51

Which of these refers to pointed teeth?

A: Bovine
B: Leonine
C: Feline
D: Canine

52

One of the tallest structures in the world is New York's Empire State... what?

A: Tower
B: Building
C: Statue
D: Column

53

Which of these creatures moves at the slowest average speed?

A: Hare
B: Cheetah
C: Greyhound
D: Sloth

54

Who removes plaque as part of his or her job?

A: Carpenter
B: Butcher
C: Dentist
D: Plumber

55

Which of these is a comic?

A: Corno
B: Beano
C: Wheato
D: Riceo

 50:50 Go to page 246   Go to page 258    ❓ Answers on page 267

6 ◆ £2,000

56

Which of these is most likely to be used by an astronomer?

- A: Kaleidoscope
- B: Telescope
- C: Stethoscope
- D: Microscope

57

Wolverine, Storm and Rogue are characters in which super-hero team?

- A: W-Men
- B: X-Men
- C: Y-Men
- D: Z-Men

58

Which of these is a traditional battle cry of American paratroopers?

- A: Sitting Bull!
- B: Hiawatha!
- C: Geronimo!
- D: Pocahontas!

page
133

59

Complete the title of the long-running TV comedy series: 'Last of the Summer...'?

- A: Sun
- B: Days
- C: Nights
- D: Wine

60

Which three letters usually precede a website address?

- A: sss
- B: www
- C: ppp
- D: mmm

50:50 Go to page 247 Go to page 258 ? Answers on page 267

6 ◆ £2,000

61

What is the name of the animated fireman on television?

A: Fireman Tim | B: Fireman Nick
C: Fireman Sam | D: Fireman Jon

62

If you wanted 'highlights', what would your hairdresser do to your hair?

A: Make it curly | B: Put in blond streaks
C: Plait it | D: Cut it short and spiky

63

Which Disney film features the song 'The Bare Necessities'?

A: Bambi | B: The Lion King
C: Pinocchio | D: The Jungle Book

64

Mint sauce is a traditional accompaniment to which meat?

A: Lamb | B: Pork
C: Beef | D: Chicken

65

In which US city is the White House?

A: New York | B: San Francisco
C: Washington DC | D: Seattle

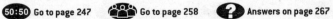

50:50 Go to page 247   Go to page 258   ? Answers on page 267

6 ◆ £2,000

66

Which of these is a TV soap?

A: Hollywillows
B: Hollyoaks
C: Hollyelms
D: Hollybirches

67

How many days are there in November?

A: 28
B: 29
C: 30
D: 31

68

Which comic book hero lives in Gotham City?

page 135

A: Superman
B: Wonder Woman
C: Aquaman
D: Batman

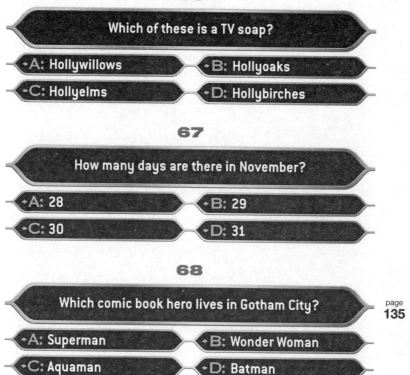

50:50 Go to page 247   Go to page 259   Answers on page 267

50:50

15	£1 MILLION
14	£500,000
13	£250,000
12	£125,000
11	£64,000
10	£32,000
9	£16,000
8	£8,000
7 ◆ £4,000
6 ◆ £2,000
5 ◆ £1,000
4 ◆ £500
3 ◆ £300
2 ◆ £200
1 ◆ £100

7 ◆ £4,000

1

Which food is mentioned in the Lord's Prayer?

A: Carrots

B: Milk

C: Bread

D: Meat

2

To which section of the orchestra does the bassoon belong?

A: Woodwind

B: Brass

C: Percussion

D: String

3

Which of these countries does not have a coastline?

A: Spain

B: France

C: Austria

D: Portugal

4

Which of these foods is produced through the process of churning?

A: Butter

B: Flour

C: Minced beef

D: Salt

5

What type of transport was the Cutty Sark?

A: Sailing ship

B: Railway train

C: Horse-drawn carriage

D: Bicycle

50:50 Go to page 247   Go to page 259   ? Answers on page 268

6

Who was the husband of Queen Victoria?

- A: Albert
- B: Arthur
- C: Alfred
- D: Arnold

7

The schilling is the unit of currency in which of these countries?

- A: Germany
- B: Canada
- C: Spain
- D: Austria

8

Which of these is a type of doctor who deals with general medical problems?

- A: PA
- B: GP
- C: QC
- D: MP

9

In which country is the city of Montreal?

- A: Scotland
- B: France
- C: Australia
- D: Canada

10

If you ordered a 'crêpe' in France, what would you expect to be served?

- A: Steak
- B: Boiled egg
- C: Pancake
- D: Glass of milk

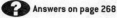 50:50 Go to page 247   Go to page 259   ? Answers on page 268

7 ◆ £4,000

11

In Arthurian legend, with whom did Sir Lancelot fall in love?

A: Gabrielle

B: Gertrude

C: Goldilocks

D: Guinevere

12

Which of these is the name of a slow-moving river of ice?

A: Drift

B: Glacier

C: Scree

D: Furrow

13

What type of creature is a stickleback?

A: Fish

B: Dog

C: Horse

D: Bear

14

In which century was World War I fought?

A: 17th

B: 18th

C: 19th

D: 20th

15

Which of these cities is located in England?

A: Norwich

B: Swansea

C: Londonderry

D: Dundee

50:50 Go to page 247　　Go to page 259　　? Answers on page 268

16

Glenn Hoddle has been a leading figure in which sport for the last 20 years?

- A: Rugby
- B: Athletics
- C: Cricket
- D: Football

17

'Ooh, Stick You' was a hit single for which teen singing duo?

- A: Doris and Cynthia
- B: Dolores and Celia
- C: Daphne and Celeste
- D: Dorothy and Celine

18

Which boy's name comes after the word 'natter' to make a breed of toad?

page
141

- A: Mike
- B: Nick
- C: Hank
- D: Jack

19

Pete Sampras is an all-time great in which sport?

- A: Basketball
- B: Baseball
- C: Golf
- D: Tennis

20

Which of these is a TV series hosted by Neil Buchanan?

- A: Take Art
- B: SMart
- C: Art Attack
- D: Watercolour Challenge

50:50 Go to page 247   Go to page 259   ? Answers on page 268

7 ◆ £4,000

21

Scandinavia is a region in which continent?

- A: Australia
- B: Africa
- C: Europe
- D: North America

22

Which of these fictional characters is the arch-enemy of Harry Potter?

- A: Darth Vader
- B: Hannibal Lecter
- C: Lord Voldemort
- D: Shredder

23

Which of these islands is also a country?

- A: Iceland
- B: Sicily
- C: Tasmania
- D: Hawaii

24

Which of these goes with 'hook' to make a fastening for clothes?

- A: Eye
- B: Ear
- C: Egg
- D: Eel

25

The coastline of Italy is on which body of water?

- A: Arabian Sea
- B: Arctic Sea
- C: Mediterranean Sea
- D: South China Sea

50:50 Go to page 247   Go to page 259   ? Answers on page 268

7 ◆ £4,000

26

'Crush On You' was a top ten hit
single for which young pop star?

◆A: Aaron Carter

◆B: Craig David

◆C: Britney Spears

◆D: Christina Aguilera

27

Which of these fractions is the largest?

◆A: $1/10$

◆B: $1/5$

◆C: $1/4$

◆D: $1/3$

28

Which animated TV character has a cat called Jess?

◆A: Kipper

◆B: Postman Pat

◆C: Noddy

◆D: Count Duckula

29

In an orchestra, which of these is one of
the main instruments of the brass section?

◆A: Greek horn

◆B: Polish horn

◆C: French horn

◆D: Indian horn

30

Paddington Bear originally came
from which part of the world?

◆A: Greenest France

◆B: Greyest Russia

◆C: Lightest India

◆D: Darkest Peru

50:50 Go to page 247   Go to page 259   ? Answers on page 268

7 ◆ £4,000

31

How many people are required to make a quintet?

A: 5
B: 6
C: 7
D: 8

32

In which mode of transport did the
Owl and the Pussycat go to sea?

A: Snow white skiff
B: Sky blue barge
C: Pea green boat
D: Blood red kayak

33

Which sport would you be practising
if you went to a driving range?

A: Clay pigeon shooting
B: Figure skating
C: Mountain climbing
D: Golf

34

'The Tale of Peter Rabbit' was the work of which author?

A: Enid Blyton
B: Beatrix Potter
C: J.K. Rowling
D: A.A. Milne

35

Tonto was the close friend and
associate of which fictional hero?

A: Dick Tracy
B: The Lone Ranger
C: The Saint
D: Biggles

 50:50 Go to page 247   Go to page 259   ? Answers on page 268

7 ◆ £4,000

36

In the film 'The Wizard of Oz', Dorothy lives in which US state?

◆A: Texas
◆B: Kansas
◆C: Alaska
◆D: Florida

37

Vienna is the capital city of which country?

◆A: Egypt
◆B: Mexico
◆C: Austria
◆D: Ireland

38

Which Disney film features the song 'That's What Friends Are For'?

◆A: The Jungle Book
◆B: Aladdin
◆C: The Lion King
◆D: Bambi

39

How many years are there in a millennium?

◆A: 50
◆B: 100
◆C: 1000
◆D: 10,000

40

Which of these princes is a nephew of Princess Anne?

◆A: Charles
◆B: William
◆C: Edward
◆D: Andrew

41

Which of these is a song from the musical 'The Sound of Music'?

- A: Seven Going on Eight
- B: Ten Going on Eleven
- C: Thirteen Going on Fourteen
- D: Sixteen Going on Seventeen

42

What type of saints are St George for England and St David for Wales?

- A: Patrol
- B: Patron
- C: Paternal
- D: Patent

43

What is a sheepshank?

- A: Flower
- B: Butterfly
- C: Knot
- D: Tool

44

Which TV soap is set in Summer Bay?

- A: Neighbours
- B: Home and Away
- C: Family Affairs
- D: Hollyoaks

45

In which month is All Fools' Day?

- A: February
- B: March
- C: April
- D: May

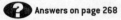
50:50 Go to page 247   Go to page 259   Answers on page 268

7 ◆ £4,000

46

What is the name of the Queen's daughter?

- A: Beatrice
- B: Anne
- C: Margaret
- D: Eugenie

47

What sort of creature is Colonel Hathi in Disney's 'The Jungle Book'?

- A: Tiger
- B: Elephant
- C: Bear
- D: Snake

48

Who wrote the book 'George's Marvellous Medicine'?

page **147**

- A: Roald Dahl
- B: A.A. Milne
- C: Enid Blyton
- D: E. Nesbit

49

The cello belongs to which section of an orchestra?

- A: String
- B: Percussion
- C: Woodwind
- D: Brass

50

Which sport has bunkers and greens?

- A: Squash
- B: Golf
- C: Motor racing
- D: Archery

50:50 Go to page 247   Go to page 259   ? Answers on page 268

7 ◆ £4,000

51

Which of these men gave his name to a temperature scale he devised?

- A: André Ampère
- B: Francis Beaufort
- C: Humphry Davy
- D: Anders Celsius

52

On TV, what type of vehicle is Brum?

- A: Car
- B: Helicopter
- C: Tugboat
- D: Bicycle

53

In athletics, what shape is the discus?

- A: Triangle
- B: Square
- C: Circle
- D: Star

54

What is the highest number in the main National Lottery draw?

- A: 49
- B: 59
- C: 69
- D: 79

55

Who wrote about Jemima Puddle-Duck and Benjamin Bunny?

- A: J.R.R. Tolkien
- B: George Eliot
- C: Enid Blyton
- D: Beatrix Potter

7 ◆ £4,000

56

In which country is the city of Adelaide?

A: China
B: Australia
C: Canada
D: Brazil

57

What is the name of the singing family in 'The Sound of Music'?

A: Von Katch
B: Von Trapp
C: Von Dropp
D: Von Trickk

58

Which of these would you need to assist you in the vault event in an athletics competition?

A: Ball
B: Pole
C: Puck
D: Bat

59

Which of these sea creatures has a dorsal fin that often protrudes out of the water?

A: Jellyfish
B: Shark
C: Octopus
D: Squid

60

Toad of Toad Hall is a character in which book?

A: The Wind in the Willows
B: The Breeze in the Beeches
C: The Gale in the Gum Trees
D: The Wisp in the Walnuts

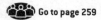 50:50 Go to page 247    Go to page 259   ? Answers on page 268

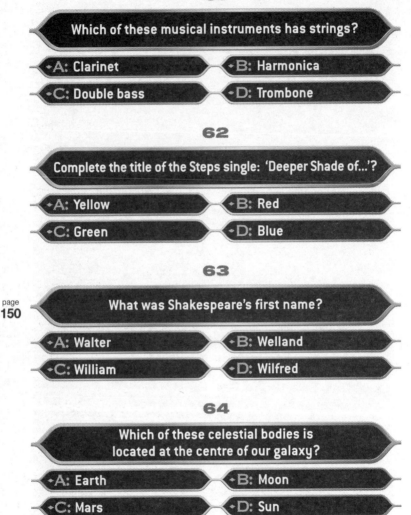

61

Which of these musical instruments has strings?

- A: Clarinet
- B: Harmonica
- C: Double bass
- D: Trombone

62

Complete the title of the Steps single: 'Deeper Shade of...'?

- A: Yellow
- B: Red
- C: Green
- D: Blue

63

What was Shakespeare's first name?

- A: Walter
- B: Welland
- C: William
- D: Wilfred

64

Which of these celestial bodies is located at the centre of our galaxy?

- A: Earth
- B: Moon
- C: Mars
- D: Sun

15   **£1 MILLION**

14   £500,000

13   £250,000

12   £125,000

11   £64,000

10   **£32,000**

9   £16,000

8 ◆ £8,000

7 ◆ £4,000

6 ◆ £2,000

5 ◆ £1,000

4 ◆ £500

3 ◆ £300

2 ◆ £200

1 ◆ £100

page
151

8 ◆ £8,000

1

Peter Parker is the secret alter-ego of which fictional superhero?

A: The Incredible Hulk
B: Spiderman
C: Wolverine
D: Captain America

2

Which European city is traditionally associated with a 'gondola'?

A: Munich
B: Barcelona
C: Nice
D: Venice

3

Which of these creatures is not a type of bird?

A: Mute swan
B: Mongoose
C: Sparrowhawk
D: Golden eagle

4

Harold Bishop is a long-standing character in which TV soap?

A: EastEnders
B: Neighbours
C: Beverly Hills 90210
D: Emmerdale

5

Which chemical element is used to purify the water in swimming pools?

A: Chlorine
B: Carbon
C: Calcium
D: Cadmium

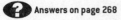
50:50 Go to page 248   Go to page 260   ? Answers on page 268

8 ◆ £8,000

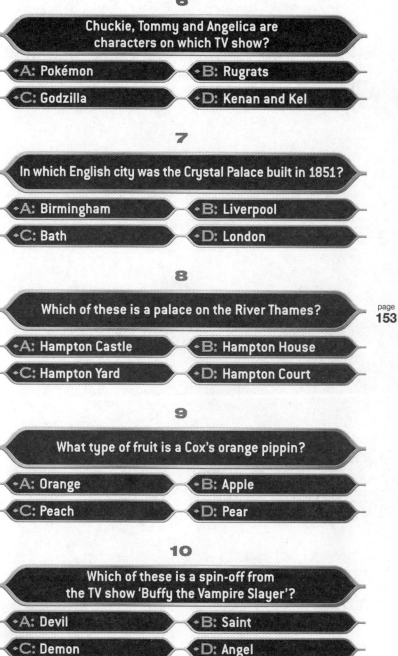

6

Chuckie, Tommy and Angelica are characters on which TV show?

- ◆A: Pokémon
- ◆B: Rugrats
- ◆C: Godzilla
- ◆D: Kenan and Kel

7

In which English city was the Crystal Palace built in 1851?

- ◆A: Birmingham
- ◆B: Liverpool
- ◆C: Bath
- ◆D: London

8

Which of these is a palace on the River Thames?

page
153

- ◆A: Hampton Castle
- ◆B: Hampton House
- ◆C: Hampton Yard
- ◆D: Hampton Court

9

What type of fruit is a Cox's orange pippin?

- ◆A: Orange
- ◆B: Apple
- ◆C: Peach
- ◆D: Pear

10

Which of these is a spin-off from the TV show 'Buffy the Vampire Slayer'?

- ◆A: Devil
- ◆B: Saint
- ◆C: Demon
- ◆D: Angel

 **50:50** Go to page 248 **Go to page 260** **?** Answers on page 268

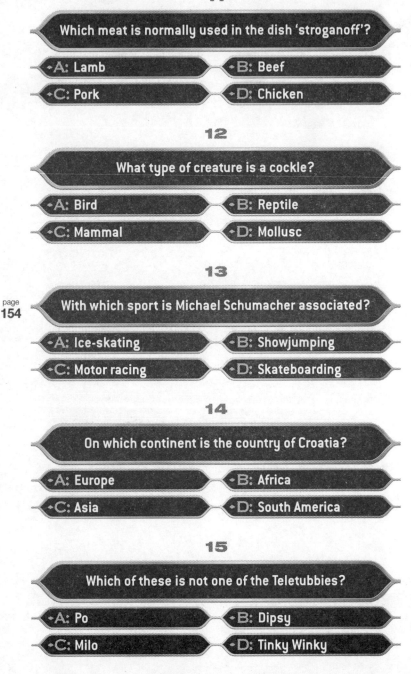

11

Which meat is normally used in the dish 'stroganoff'?

- A: Lamb
- B: Beef
- C: Pork
- D: Chicken

12

What type of creature is a cockle?

- A: Bird
- B: Reptile
- C: Mammal
- D: Mollusc

13

With which sport is Michael Schumacher associated?

- A: Ice-skating
- B: Showjumping
- C: Motor racing
- D: Skateboarding

14

On which continent is the country of Croatia?

- A: Europe
- B: Africa
- C: Asia
- D: South America

15

Which of these is not one of the Teletubbies?

- A: Po
- B: Dipsy
- C: Milo
- D: Tinky Winky

 50:50 Go to page 248   Go to page 260   ? Answers on page 268

8 ◆ £8,000

16

What mode of transport is a limousine?

- A: Train
- B: Car
- C: Hovercraft
- D: Bicycle

17

Which of these is the title of a popular book and BBC TV series?

- A: The Devil Headmaster
- B: The Demon Headmistress
- C: The Satanic Housemaster
- D: The Demon Headmaster

18

In which of these sports would you use a 'cue' to strike the ball?

page **155**

- A: Football
- B: Tennis
- C: Hockey
- D: Snooker

19

Which of these is a lightly perfumed liquid similar to cologne?

- A: Tonic water
- B: Dish water
- C: Toilet water
- D: Bath water

20

The Zulu people originate from which continent?

- A: Africa
- B: Asia
- C: South America
- D: Australia

50:50 Go to page 248   Go to page 260   ? Answers on page 268

8 ◆ £8,000

21

Which 'Teenage Witch' is friends
with a talking black cat named Salem?

A: Selena

B: Samantha

C: Sabrina

D: Serena

22

In which part of the UK is the royal residence of Balmoral?

A: Scotland

B: Wales

C: Northern Ireland

D: England

23

'Rollercoaster' and 'C'est La Vie'
were hit singles for which band?

A: Steps

B: Westlife

C: S Club 7

D: B*Witched

24

Which of these is a popular daily newspaper in Britain?

A: Sun

B: Sunday Times

C: Observer

D: Oracle

25

Excluding substitutes, how many players
are there in a standard football team?

A: 10

B: 11

C: 13

D: 15

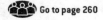 50:50 Go to page 248   Go to page 260   ? Answers on page 268

8 ◆ £8,000

26

Which of these countries has the largest surface area?

◆A: France
◆B: Canada
◆C: Denmark
◆D: Ecuador

27

What do barristers often have to wear on their heads while appearing in court?

◆A: Baseball caps
◆B: Top hats
◆C: Trilbies
◆D: Wigs

28

What would you traditionally do with a tankard?

◆A: Drink from it
◆B: Paint with it
◆C: Wear it
◆D: See through it

29

Which animated TV show is set in the town of Springfield?

◆A: South Park
◆B: The Simpsons
◆C: The Flintstones
◆D: King of the Hill

30

Which of these tools would you use to check whether a surface was straight?

◆A: Hammer
◆B: Spirit level
◆C: Screwdriver
◆D: Chisel

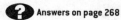 **50:50** Go to page 248   **Go to page 260**   **?** Answers on page 268

8 ◆ £8,000

31

Which of these people is credited with the discovery of the West Indies in 1492?

- A: Christopher Columbus
- B: Christopher Cazenove
- C: Christopher Lee
- D: Christopher Biggins

32

Which of these goes with St Pancras to make a London Underground station?

- A: King's Cross
- B: Queen's Cross
- C: Prince's Cross
- D: Duke's Cross

33

'As Long As You Love Me' and 'I Want It That Way' were hit singles for which boy band?

- A: *NSYNC
- B: New Kids On The Block
- C: Backstreet Boys
- D: Hanson

34

Which of these was not a member of the boy band Take That?

- A: Brian Harvey
- B: Mark Owen
- C: Gary Barlow
- D: Howard Donald

35

Who played Batman in the 1997 film 'Batman and Robin'?

- A: Mel Gibson
- B: George Clooney
- C: Alec Baldwin
- D: Richard Gere

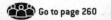 50:50 Go to page 248   Go to page 260    ? Answers on page 268

8 ◆ £8,000

36

Which of these is a classic Chinese speciality?

A: Bird's nest soup

B: Rabbit's warren soup

C: Horse's stable soup

D: Cat's basket soup

37

What are 'galoshes'?

A: Ear protectors

B: Sunglasses

C: False fingernails

D: Waterproof shoes

38

Which obelisk was given to Britain by Egypt in the 1870s and now stands on the River Thames?

page 159

A: Cleopatra's Tower

B: Cleopatra's Bridge

C: Cleopatra's Needle

D: Cleopatra's Crown

39

'Look at Me' was the debut solo single of which of the Spice Girls?

A: Melanie Chisholm

B: Emma Bunton

C: Geri Halliwell

D: Victoria Beckham

40

Sinus problems relate to which part of the human body?

A: Feet

B: Back

C: Nose

D: Hands

50:50 Go to page 248   Go to page 260   ? Answers on page 268

8 ◆ £8,000

41

Which of these was a famous explorer in Elizabethan England?

◆A: Francis Mallard | ◆B: Francis Swan
◆C: Francis Goose | ◆D: Francis Drake

42

Which infamous tourist attraction was built in the part of London known as Greenwich?

◆A: Big Ben | ◆B: Hampton Court
◆C: Millennium Dome | ◆D: London Eye

43

Which TV quiz show is hosted by William G. Stewart?

◆A: Ten to One | ◆B: Twelve to One
◆C: Fifteen to One | ◆D: Twenty to One

44

Which king of England won the Battle of Hastings?

◆A: Richard the Lionheart | ◆B: William the Conqueror
◆C: William of Orange | ◆D: Alfred the Great

45

In the award-winning short film 'The Wrong Trousers', what is the name of Wallace's dog?

◆A: Rover | ◆B: Crookshanks
◆C: Gromit | ◆D: Timmy

50:50 Go to page 248   Go to page 260   ? Answers on page 268

46

What kind of food is a mango?

A: Fruit
B: Herb
C: Fish
D: Spice

47

Which film musical features the song 'The Lonely Goatherd'?

A: Mary Poppins
B: The Wizard of Oz
C: Chitty Chitty Bang Bang
D: The Sound of Music

48

How are Lakes Superior, Michigan, Huron, Erie and Ontario collectively known?

page **161**

A: The Good Lakes
B: The Glorious Lakes
C: The Great Lakes
D: The Groovy Lakes

49

Which of these is a former British prime minister?

A: Bill Clinton
B: John Major
C: Morgan Freeman
D: Florence Nightingale

50

Which planet shares its name with a cartoon dog?

A: Neptune
B: Saturn
C: Pluto
D: Mercury

50:50 Go to page 248   Go to page 260   ? Answers on page 268

8 ◆ £8,000

51

Which city hosted the 2000 Olympic Games?

- A: Sydney
- B: Athens
- C: Melbourne
- D: Tokyo

52

What type of TV programme is associated with the phrase 'Looney Tunes'?

- A: Chat shows
- B: Cartoons
- C: Cookery programmes
- D: Game shows

53

Which of these are essential for a game of 'whist'?

- A: Bats
- B: Balls
- C: Cards
- D: Marbles

54

In the TV comedy 'Friends', whose surname is Buffay?

- A: Rachel
- B: Joey
- C: Chandler
- D: Phoebe

55

To which pop group did the singer Louise originally belong?

- A: All Saints
- B: Precious
- C: Spice Girls
- D: Eternal

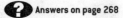 50:50 Go to page 248   Go to page 260   ? Answers on page 268

8 ◆ £8,000

56

Complete this proverb: 'A bird in the hand is worth two in the...'?

- A: Bush
- B: Hedge
- C: Tree
- D: Nest

57

What is the name of Prince Edward's sister?

- A: Sophie
- B: Elizabeth
- C: Anne
- D: Sarah

58

Which characters appear in the animated film 'A Close Shave'?

- A: Bodger and Badger
- B: Wallace and Gromit
- C: Rosie and Jim
- D: Sooty and Sweep

59

In which month is St George's Day?

- A: April
- B: May
- C: November
- D: December

60

In which novel does Tiny Tim appear?

- A: A Christmas Carol
- B: David Copperfield
- C: Oliver Twist
- D: A Tale of Two Cities

50:50 Go to page 248   Go to page 260   ? Answers on page 268

50:50

15	**£1 MILLION**
14	£500,000
13	£250,000
12	£125,000
11	£64,000
10	£32,000
9 ◆	**£16,000**
8 ◆	£8,000
7 ◆	£4,000
6 ◆	£2,000
5 ◆	£1,000
4 ◆	£500
3 ◆	£300
2 ◆	£200
1 ◆	£100

9 ◆ £16,000

1

In which film did Mel Gibson play a rooster named Rocky?

A: Chicken Run
B: Hen Charge
C: Fowl Trot
D: Cock Sprint

2

What architectural oddity is located in the Italian town of Pisa?

A: Sagging Bridge
B: Cracking Arch
C: Leaning Tower
D: Smelly Drains

3

Humpback and orca are varieties of which sea creature?

A: Whale
B: Starfish
C: Sea horse
D: Octopus

4

Which of these is a unit of computer memory?

A: Megamunch
B: Meganibble
C: Megabyte
D: Megasnack

5

Who was Tutankhamen?

A: Roman emperor
B: Egyptian pharaoh
C: British king
D: American president

50:50 Go to page 248　　Go to page 260　　? Answers on page 268

9 ◆ £16,000

6

Which of these animals is well-known for giving off a foul smell if threatened?

- A: Cat
- B: Sheep
- C: Pig
- D: Skunk

7

Which of these released the album 'Right Now' in 2000?

- A: Sugababes
- B: Jennifer Lopez
- C: Atomic Kitten
- D: Sonique

8

Which king is associated with the mythical kingdom of Camelot?

- A: King Henry
- B: King Alfred
- C: King Edward
- D: King Arthur

9

What does the letter 'D' stand for in the phrase 3-D?

- A: Directional
- B: Deviational
- C: Dimensional
- D: Diagonal

10

A stag is the adult male of which animal?

- A: Horse
- B: Deer
- C: Sheep
- D: Goat

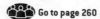 50:50 Go to page 248   Go to page 260   Answers on page 268

9 ◆ £16,000

11

What name was given to slaves trained to fight each other for entertainment in the Roman Empire?

- A: Senators
- B: Gladiators
- C: Centurions
- D: Decurions

12

Complete the title of the Robert Louis Stevenson novel: 'Treasure...'?

- A: Place
- B: Country
- C: Island
- D: Region

13

What type of animal is a puffin?

- A: Fish
- B: Bird
- C: Sheep
- D: Tiger

14

What can you specifically do if you are ambidextrous?

- A: Speak two languages
- B: Play the piano
- C: Write with both hands
- D: Swim underwater

15

What name is given to the young of a kangaroo?

- A: Jimmy
- B: Jamie
- C: Jodie
- D: Joey

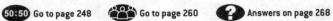 50:50 Go to page 248   Go to page 260   ? Answers on page 268

9 ◆ £16,000

16

Which monument stands in London's Trafalgar Square?

A: Wellington's Column
B: Churchill's Column
C: Nelson's Column
D: Monty's Column

17

Craig, Sada, Darren and Anna were competitors in which TV show in the summer of 2000?

A: Fat Father
B: Small Sister
C: Big Brother
D: Cute Cousin

18

The Titanic sank in 1912 after colliding with what object?

page 169

A: Blue whale
B: Cruise liner
C: Iceberg
D: Submarine

19

Which major war took place between 1939 and 1945?

A: Crimean
B: Boer
C: World War II
D: Vietnam War

20

What is the name of the stick used by the conductor of an orchestra?

A: Bradawl
B: Baton
C: Shillelagh
D: Cosh

50:50 Go to page 248   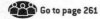 Go to page 261    ? Answers on page 268

21

Which part of Pinocchio's anatomy grew when he told a lie?

- A: Feet
- B: Hands
- C: Nose
- D: Ears

22

Who was the star of the Disney film 'Flubber'?

- A: Eddie Murphy
- B: Robin Williams
- C: Jim Carrey
- D: Rick Moranis

23

Which biblical character had his hair cut by Delilah?

- A: Solomon
- B: Simon
- C: Saul
- D: Samson

24

Delia Smith is a leading expert on which subject?

- A: Gardening
- B: DIY
- C: Antiques
- D: Cookery

25

Which part of the body is most affected by a migraine?

- A: Heart
- B: Head
- C: Kidney
- D: Teeth

50:50 Go to page 249   Go to page 261   ? Answers on page 268

9 ◆ £16,000

26

How are Buttercup, Blossom and Bubbles collectively known in the cartoon world?

A: The Powerpuff Girls
B: The Tigertuff Girls
C: The Superstuff Girls
D: The Flowerfluff Girls

27

Which of these is a bird that cannot fly but is able to run very fast?

A: Eagle
B: Penguin
C: Ostrich
D: Condor

28

Who was the star of the TV sitcom 'The Fresh Prince of Bel Air'?

page 171

A: Eddie Murphy
B: Martin Lawrence
C: Chris Rock
D: Will Smith

29

Muhammad Ali was a world champion in which sport?

A: Athletics
B: Boxing
C: Motor racing
D: Table tennis

30

In the TV series 'Angel', what type of creature is the title character?

A: Vampire
B: Warlock
C: Werewolf
D: Ghoul

9 ◆ £16,000

31

A 'geyser' is a type of what?

A: Spring

B: Summer

C: Autumn

D: Winter

32

Which word meaning to jump around in a happy way is also a flower bud used to flavour food?

A: Prance

B: Caper

C: Gambol

D: Jig

33

In which country is the Acropolis?

A: France

B: Spain

C: Italy

D: Greece

34

Which of these describes an unlikely explanation?

A: Far-fetched

B: Far East

C: By far

D: So far

35

What do Americans traditionally eat on Thanksgiving Day?

A: Turkey

B: Beef

C: Pork

D: Fish

50:50 Go to page 249 Go to page 261 ? Answers on page 268

9 ◆ £16,000

36

How many years are there in three quarters of a century?

A: 25
B: 50
C: 75
D: 100

37

What type of food is a 'chipolata'?

A: Vegetable
B: Fruit
C: Sausage
D: Nut

38

Which of these was used for chariot racing in ancient Rome?

page 173

A: Palindrome
B: Hippodrome
C: Aerodrome
D: Velodrome

39

What is the name of Harry Potter's owl?

A: Cornelius
B: Ravenclaw
C: Hedwig
D: Hagrid

40

In France, what is a 'boulanger'?

A: Milkman
B: Baker
C: Butcher
D: Greengrocer

50:50 Go to page 249   Go to page 261   ? Answers on page 268

9 ◆ £16,000

41

What is the subject of TV programmes presented by Sir Patrick Moore?

- A: Cookery
- B: Motoring
- C: Astronomy
- D: Gardening

42

Complete the title of the Julia Roberts film: 'My Best Friend's...'?

- A: Wedding
- B: Birthday
- C: Funeral
- D: Dog

43

David Seaman has represented England in which sport?

- A: Football
- B: Cricket
- C: Rugby union
- D: Golf

44

Which of these is one of the Tweenies?

- A: Fizz
- B: Buzz
- C: Jazz
- D: Rozz

45

Which term refers to someone or something from the planet Mars?

- A: Mardian
- B: Marlian
- C: Martian
- D: Marsian

50:50 Go to page 249   Go to page 261   **?** Answers on page 268

9 ◆ £16,000

46

In the Old Testament, who slayed the giant Goliath?

- A: Joshua
- B: Simeon
- C: David
- D: Peter

47

'Raiders of the Lost Ark' was the first in a series of films to feature which hero?

- A: Batman
- B: Ace Ventura
- C: Indiana Jones
- D: Austin Powers

48

Which parts of the body do crickets rub together to make their distinctive chirping sound?

- A: Back legs
- B: Front wings
- C: Antennae
- D: Tail and head

49

From which part of the world did the Vikings come?

- A: Scandinavia
- B: Greece
- C: Antarctica
- D: Caribbean

50

Which of these is a type of fabric?

- A: Cordial
- B: Corduroy
- C: Cordierite
- D: Cordoba

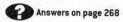 50:50 Go to page 249   Go to page 261   ? Answers on page 268

51

What is the tallest land animal in the world?

A: Elephant
B: Giraffe
C: Hippopotamus
D: Buffalo

52

What was the first name of the writer Kipling?

A: Ronald
B: Rudyard
C: Richard
D: Robert

53

Which of these is a ballet skirt?

A: Tutu
B: Pirouette
C: Pas de deux
D: Entrechat

54

Which sport is featured in the US TV series 'Hang Time'?

A: Baseball
B: Ice hockey
C: American football
D: Basketball

55

Which country is associated with 'castanets'?

A: Spain
B: France
C: Australia
D: China

50:50 Go to page 249   Go to page 261   ? Answers on page 268

56

Bald and golden are types of which bird?

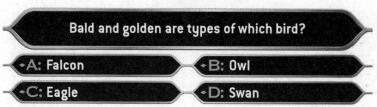

A: Falcon

B: Owl

C: Eagle

D: Swan

50:50 Go to page 249   Go to page 261   **?** Answers on page 268

15	**£1 MILLION**
14	£500,000
13	£250,000
12	£125,000
11	£64,000
10 ◆	**£32,000**
9 ◆	£16,000
8 ◆	£8,000
7 ◆	£4,000
6 ◆	£2,000
5 ◆	**£1,000**
4 ◆	£500
3 ◆	£300
2 ◆	£200
1 ◆	£100

page 179

10 ◆ £32,000

1

Which famous scientist formulated the theory of relativity in 1905?

- A: Stephen Hawking
- B: Albert Einstein
- C: Isaac Newton
- D: Louis Pasteur

2

What is the name for the Japanese art of paper folding?

- A: Karate
- B: Origami
- C: Feng shui
- D: Taekwondo

3

What name is given to a feather dipped in ink and used as a pen?

- A: Quibble
- B: Quiff
- C: Quill
- D: Quip

4

Which of these birds is a large black member of the crow family?

- A: Heron
- B: Robin
- C: Raven
- D: Albatross

5

What type of protective clothing was a gauntlet?

- A: Helmet
- B: Glove
- C: Boot
- D: Gumshield

50:50 Go to page 249   Go to page 261   ? Answers on page 269

10 ◆ £32,000

6

Which of these would be most likely to use a 'barre'?

A: Portrait painter | B: Ballet dancer
C: Classical guitarist | D: Stand-up comedian

7

What kind of weapon is traditionally kept in a 'scabbard'?

A: Arrow | B: Spear
C: Mace | D: Sword

8

In 'Coronation Street', who had a baby called Bethany in 2000?

A: Toyah Battersby | B: Sarah Louise Platt
C: Hayley Cropper | D: Linda Sykes

9

How many major planets are there in the solar system?

A: Five | B: Nine
C: Fifteen | D: Twenty

10

Which of these devices would be most likely to be used by a doctor?

A: Spirit level | B: Tuning fork
C: Telescope | D: Stethoscope

50:50 Go to page 249   Go to page 261   ? Answers on page 269

11

The Incan civilization was based in which continent?

- A: South America
- B: Europe
- C: Asia
- D: Antarctica

12

What is a glockenspiel?

- A: Breed of dog
- B: Musical instrument
- C: Carriage clock
- D: Aeroplane

13

Which two members of Steps present the TV show 'Steps to the Stars'?

- A: Claire and H
- B: Lisa and Claire
- C: Lisa and Lee
- D: Lee and H

14

The hippopotamus is native to which continent?

- A: Europe
- B: Africa
- C: South America
- D: Asia

15

Which of these animals has ten limbs?

- A: Spider
- B: Beetle
- C: Octopus
- D: Lobster

50:50 Go to page 249   Go to page 261   ? Answers on page 269

10 ◆ £32,000

16

Goodison Park is the home ground of which football team?

- A: Chelsea
- B: Crystal Palace
- C: Everton
- D: Leeds United

17

'Greengage' is a variety of which fruit?

- A: Apple
- B: Orange
- C: Plum
- D: Strawberry

18

Los Angeles is a city in which American state?

- A: Texas
- B: Florida
- C: Mississippi
- D: California

19

What was the first name of the Spanish painter Picasso?

- A: Pietro
- B: Pablo
- C: Philippe
- D: Patrice

20

How many wives did King Henry VIII of England have?

- A: 4
- B: 5
- C: 6
- D: 7

50:50 Go to page 249   Go to page 261   **?** Answers on page 269

10 ◆ £32,000

21

In London, what are Claridges, the Savoy and the Ritz?

- A: Hotels
- B: Toy museums
- C: Underground stations
- D: Department stores

22

What type of creature is a marmot?

- A: Bird
- B: Snake
- C: Fish
- D: Rodent

23

With which country are Maori people associated?

- A: Canada
- B: New Zealand
- C: South Africa
- D: Republic of Ireland

24

Boris Becker was a leading figure in which sport?

- A: Football
- B: Basketball
- C: Tennis
- D: Athletics

25

Which of these is a condiment?

- A: Knife
- B: Mustard
- C: Lettuce
- D: Cornflakes

50:50 Go to page 249   Go to page 261   ? Answers on page 269

10 ◆ £32,000

26

Which of these sports uses tramlines?

- A: Basketball
- B: Lawn tennis
- C: Squash
- D: Volleyball

27

As what did Margot Fonteyn become famous?

- A: Opera singer
- B: Ballerina
- C: Painter
- D: Author

28

Bobbie and Phyllis belong to which of these groups?

page
185

- A: The Railway Children
- B: The Secret Seven
- C: The Famous Five
- D: The Magnificent Seven

29

Which of these birds can't fly?

- A: Emu
- B: Jackdaw
- C: Peacock
- D: Goose

30

Which drink is particularly associated with the Indian town of Darjeeling?

- A: Cocoa
- B: Tea
- C: Coffee
- D: Orange squash

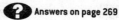
50:50 Go to page 249   Go to page 261   ? Answers on page 269

10 ◆ £32,000

31

Which of these is a tuft of hair that will not lie down?

A: Piglick
B: Cowlick
C: Henlick
D: Sheeplick

32

Which instrument would normally be used to play honky-tonk ragtime music?

A: Trumpet
B: Saxophone
C: Double bass
D: Piano

page
186

33

Who was on the throne at the time of the Great Exhibition in 1851?

A: William IV
B: Victoria
C: Edward VII
D: George VI

34

What was the nationality of the composer Beethoven?

A: English
B: French
C: Danish
D: German

35

Hammerhead and thresher are varieties of which sea creature?

A: Urchin
B: Prawn
C: Shark
D: Seal

10 ◆ £32,000

36

Ian Botham is a former England captain at which sport?

- A: Football
- B: Rugby union
- C: Cricket
- D: Tennis

37

Which of these would be involved in a drag race?

- A: Dog
- B: Horse
- C: Pigeon
- D: Car

38

Which of these is the hair obtained from angora goats?

- A: Rohair
- B: Bohair
- C: Mohair
- D: Sohair

39

Which British coin features a lion?

- A: 1p
- B: 2p
- C: 5p
- D: 10p

40

Which pop duo had a UK top ten hit in 1998 with 'Truly Madly Deeply'?

- A: Spiteful Patio
- B: Vicious Arbour
- C: Merciless Allotment
- D: Savage Garden

50:50 Go to page 249　　Go to page 261　　**?** Answers on page 269

10 ♦ £32,000

41

Which monarch reigned in both
the 19th and 20th centuries?

A: William IV
B: George V
C: Edward VII
D: Victoria

42

In which sport is Lee Westwood a leading figure?

A: Golf
B: Snooker
C: Bowls
D: Darts

43

By what first name was the singer
Harry Lillis Crosby better known?

A: Sting
B: Spring
C: Bing
D: Thing

44

What colour are the berries on a mistletoe plant?

A: Black
B: Red
C: Orange
D: White

45

Who did William the Conqueror
defeat at the Battle of Hastings?

A: Harold II
B: Philip II
C: Richard II
D: John II

50:50 Go to page 250   Go to page 262   ? Answers on page 269

10 ◆ £32,000

46

The tennis player Greg Rusedski was born in which country?

A: Canada | B: Mexico
C: Brazil | D: Argentina

47

Which Hollywood action man played the boxer Rocky Balboa in a series of films?

A: Arnold Schwarzenegger | B: Bruce Willis
C: Sylvester Stallone | D: Jean-Claude Van Damme

48

What type of creature is an elk?

page
189

A: Lizard | B: Rodent
C: Deer | D: Beetle

49

Which novel by Jamila Gavin won the Whitbread children's book of the year prize in 2001?

A: Coram Boy | B: Coram Girl
C: Coram Man | D: Coram Woman

50

To which country does the island of Corfu belong?

A: Spain | B: Italy
C: France | D: Greece

50:50 Go to page 250   Go to page 262   Answers on page 269

51

What is 60% written as a fraction?

A: 3/8

B: 3/4

C: 3/5

D: 3/10

52

The Superbowl is the highlight of the season in which sport?

A: American football

B: Baseball

C: Ice hockey

D: Basketball

50:50 Go to page 250   Go to page 262   ? Answers on page 269

15	£1 MILLION
14	£500,000
13	£250,000
12	£125,000
11 ◆	£64,000
10 ◆	£32,000
9 ◆	£16,000
8 ◆	£8,000
7 ◆	£4,000
6 ◆	£2,000
5 ◆	£1,000
4 ◆	£500
3 ◆	£300
2 ◆	£200
1 ◆	£100

11 ◆ £64,000

1

Which people of Penzance feature in the title of a Gilbert and Sullivan operetta?

A: The Peasants

B: The Puppeteers

C: The Priests

D: The Pirates

2

In which continent are Zambia and Zimbabwe?

A: Africa

B: Europe

C: Asia

D: Australia

3

Who won the 1998 men's football world cup?

A: England

B: Germany

C: Brazil

D: France

4

Which car manufacturer produced the Prefect, Anglia and Cortina?

A: Ford

B: Renault

C: Vauxhall

D: Rover

5

Portugal shares a border with which other European country?

A: Greece

B: Denmark

C: Spain

D: Norway

50:50 Go to page 250   Go to page 262   ? Answers on page 269

6

What type of animal is a dolphin?

A: Bird
B: Reptile
C: Mammal
D: Mollusc

7

What is the name of the princess in the Disney animated film 'Aladdin'?

A: Violet
B: Jasmine
C: Saffron
D: Lavender

8

The 'samurai' were a type of ancient warrior based in which country?

A: Japan
B: Mexico
C: Egypt
D: Greece

9

In Greek mythology, who had to complete twelve difficult labours?

A: Jupiter
B: Heracles
C: Achilles
D: Hermes

10

Which of these words means one after another without interruption?

A: Penultimate
B: Symmetrical
C: Consecutive
D: Cylindrical

11 ◆ £64,000

11

What is the capital of Italy?

A: Turin
B: Naples
C: Milan
D: Rome

12

Precipitation is another name for which type of weather?

A: Thunder
B: Heatwave
C: Hurricane
D: Rain

13

Harry Houdini was famous for what?

A: Painting
B: Sport
C: Escapology
D: Science

14

Which of these is one of the children who visit Willy Wonka's Chocolate Factory in Roald Dahl's book?

A: Vanity Vinegar
B: Veruca Salt
C: Verity Pepper
D: Variety Mustard

15

A heifer is a young what?

A: Horse
B: Cow
C: Goose
D: Goat

50:50 Go to page 250   Go to page 262   **?** Answers on page 269

11 ◆ £64,000

16

Which of these countries is in Australasia?

A: New Zealand   B: South Africa

C: Canada   D: India

17

'Nouvelle cuisine' is a style of what?

A: Pottery   B: Cookery

C: Carpentry   D: Archery

18

When England and Australia play each other at cricket, what trophy do they compete for?

page **195**

A: The Wisden Trophy   B: The Sheffield Shield

C: The Ashes   D: The Melbourne Cup

19

In which month is Remembrance Sunday?

A: June   B: September

C: November   D: March

20

Manhattan is a borough of which US city?

A: Los Angeles   B: Chicago

C: Miami   D: New York

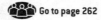

11 ◆ £64,000

21

Which of the following is a member of the pop group Five?

- A: Pecs
- B: Abs
- C: Six-Pack
- D: Hamstring

22

What type of creature is a 'gecko'?

- A: Insect
- B: Lizard
- C: Snake
- D: Bird

23

'Ray of Light' and 'Music' are recent albums by which singer?

- A: Britney Spears
- B: Shania Twain
- C: Madonna
- D: Louise

24

Which of these words means a small group of trees?

- A: Hopse
- B: Dopse
- C: Copse
- D: Fopse

25

What name is given to an afternoon rest, usually taken by inhabitants of hot countries such as Spain?

- A: Fiesta
- B: Sangria
- C: Andalucia
- D: Siesta

50:50 Go to page 250   Go to page 262   ? Answers on page 269

11 ◆ £64,000

26

Which of these is a variety of aquatic bird?

- A: Coot
- B: Toot
- C: Root
- D: Noot

27

Professor Moriarty is the arch-enemy of which fictional detective?

- A: Inspector Morse
- B: Sherlock Holmes
- C: Hercule Poirot
- D: Miss Marple

28

Hollywood is a suburb of which US city?

- A: Chicago
- B: Los Angeles
- C: New York
- D: Washington

29

Who was at the centre of the Gunpowder Plot?

- A: Thomas Blood
- B: Kim Philby
- C: George Blunt
- D: Guy Fawkes

30

Which of these islands is also a country?

- A: Cuba
- B: Anglesey
- C: Corsica
- D: Crete

50:50 Go to page 250   Go to page 262   ? Answers on page 269

11 ◆ £64,000

31

In the Bible, who was arrested
in the Garden of Gethsemane?

- A: Noah
- B: Abraham
- C: Jesus
- D: Moses

32

What is the name of the Wimbledon 2000
champion, whose surname is Williams?

- A: Venus
- B: Diana
- C: Minerva
- D: Juno

33

Which of these musical instruments does not have a reed?

- A: Piccolo
- B: Clarinet
- C: Saxophone
- D: Oboe

34

Which of these counties does not border Devon?

- A: Cornwall
- B: Somerset
- C: Hampshire
- D: Dorset

35

What was the first name of the
Victorian prime minister Gladstone?

- A: Walter
- B: William
- C: Wilfred
- D: Winston

50:50 Go to page 250 Go to page 262 ? Answers on page 269

11 ◆ £64,000

36

In France, what is a 'lycée'?

- A: Secondary school
- B: Hospital
- C: Theatre
- D: Post office

37

What type of creature is a 'whiting'?

- A: Bird
- B: Snake
- C: Insect
- D: Fish

38

Which character from Greek mythology gives his name to a tendon in the leg?

- A: Heracles
- B: Achilles
- C: Perseus
- D: Theseus

39

In which continent is Mount Everest?

- A: Asia
- B: Europe
- C: Australia
- D: Africa

40

What is a conundrum?

- A: Geographical feature
- B: Musical instrument
- C: Type of biscuit
- D: Difficult problem

50:50 Go to page 250   Go to page 262   Answers on page 269

11 ◆ £64,000

41

On TV, who became the host
of 'The Weakest Link' in 2000?

A: Anne Robinson

B: Les Dennis

C: Richard Whiteley

D: Cilla Black

42

Which of these foods are traditionally
eaten on Shrove Tuesday?

A: Pancakes

B: Easter eggs

C: Hot cross buns

D: Christmas cakes

43

Johannesburg and Durban are cities in which country?

A: Sweden

B: South Africa

C: Brazil

D: Canada

44

Which of these sports does not use a net?

A: Table tennis

B: Badminton

C: Volleyball

D: Rounders

45

Stockholm and Frankfurt are cities on which continent?

A: Africa

B: Asia

C: Europe

D: Australia

50:50 Go to page 250   Go to page 262   ? Answers on page 269

11 ◆ £64,000

46

Which of these is not a Shakespeare play?

- A: Twelfth Night
- B: The Tragedy of Errors
- C: King Lear
- D: As You Like It

47

A pedicurist looks after which part of the body?

- A: Eyes
- B: Hair
- C: Feet
- D: Ears

48

Which Italian city is famous for its canals?

page
201

- A: Rome
- B: Pisa
- C: Florence
- D: Venice

50:50 Go to page 250   Go to page 262   **?** Answers on page 269

50:50		

15 **£1 MILLION**

14 £500,000

13 £250,000

12 ◆ £125,000

11 ◆ £64,000

10 ◆ £32,000

9 ◆ £16,000

8 ◆ £8,000

7 ◆ £4,000

6 ◆ £2,000

5 ◆ £1,000

4 ◆ £500

3 ◆ £300

2 ◆ £200

1 ◆ £100

1

Which of these units of length is the shortest?

A: Hand

B: Fathom

C: Mile

D: Foot

2

Aborigines are native to which country?

A: Australia

B: United States

C: Mexico

D: Peru

3

Which of these is a type of robot?

A: Andesite

B: Android

C: Angara

D: Anecdote

4

What name is given to someone
who has no belief in God or gods?

A: Athos

B: Atheist

C: Athenian

D: Athlete

5

What was the first name of the artist van Gogh?

A: Valentine

B: Victor

C: Vasco

D: Vincent

12 ◆ £125,000

6

Which of these would be found on almost any item bought from a supermarket?

A: Bar graph

B: Bar fly

C: Bar code

D: Bar line

7

Beige is a shade of which colour?

A: Pink

B: Blue

C: Green

D: Brown

8

Which chesspiece can only move diagonally?

A: Knight

B: Castle

C: Bishop

D: Pawn

9

'Bonsai' is the art of growing small, ornamental... what?

A: Insects

B: Fish

C: Trees

D: Fungi

10

Which famous artist painted the Mona Lisa?

A: Michelangelo

B: Leonardo da Vinci

C: Raphael

D: Botticelli

 50:50 Go to page 250   Go to page 262   ? Answers on page 269

12 ◆ £125,000

Which of these would be most likely to use a metronome?

- A: Musician
- B: Surgeon
- C: Architect
- D: Computer programmer

12

What is the main diet of a panda?

- A: Acorns
- B: Bamboo
- C: Rodents
- D: Insects

13

Which of these is a synonym of the word 'cold'?

- A: Hot
- B: Chilly
- C: Clod
- D: Old

14

Balsa is a lightweight variety of what?

- A: Wood
- B: Iron
- C: Granite
- D: Paper

15

Which of these films was made by the 'Four Weddings and a Funeral' team?

- A: The Full Monty
- B: Billy Elliot
- C: Notting Hill
- D: Little Voice

50:50 Go to page 251   Go to page 263   Answers on page 269

12 ◆ £125,000

16

Byrne is the surname of which member of Westlife?

A: Nicky
B: Shane
C: Bryan
D: Mark

17

Which type of bird has varieties called Emperor, Galapagos and Rockhopper?

A: Penguin
B: Eagle
C: Raven
D: Thrush

18

In the novel 'Around the World in Eighty Days', what is the surname of the character Phileas?

A: Misst
B: Fogg
C: Rainn
D: Snoe

19

Which of these is a type of poisonous sea creature?

A: Spanish man-of-war
B: Portuguese man-of-war
C: Italian man-of-war
D: German man-of-war

20

Who plays the role of Mr Bean on TV and film?

A: Rowan Atkinson
B: Harry Enfield
C: Paul Whitehouse
D: Charlie Higson

50:50 Go to page 251   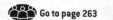 Go to page 263   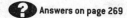 Answers on page 269

21

Which singer played Miguel Morez
in the US soap 'General Hospital'?

A: Ronan Keating
B: Ricky Martin
C: Robbie Williams
D: Ritchie Neville

22

In the cartoon 'Pokémon', what number is Charmander?

A: 4
B: 10
C: 16
D: 18

23

Which of these Roman numerals
represents the number forty?

A: XD
B: XC
C: XM
D: XL

24

In the TV series 'Star Trek: Voyager',
who is the captain of the ship?

A: Benjamin Sisko
B: Jean-Luc Picard
C: Kathryn Janeway
D: James T. Kirk

25

Which fictitious monster was fought by
Brendan Fraser and Rachel Weisz in a 1998 film?

A: The Vampire
B: The Mummy
C: The Wolfman
D: The Yeti

50:50 Go to page 251   Go to page 263   ? Answers on page 269

12 ◆ £125,000

26

What is the main unit of currency in Greece?

A: Peso

B: Drachma

C: Dollar

D: Franc

27

Who played the role of Obi-Wan Kenobi in 'Star Wars Episode One: The Phantom Menace'?

A: Ewan McGregor

B: Harrison Ford

C: Liam Neeson

D: Jake Lloyd

28

What was the first name of the scientist Fleming who discovered penicillin?

A: Arthur

B: Alexander

C: Aubrey

D: Alistair

29

Which mythical creature only appears at a full moon and can be killed by a silver bullet?

A: Vampire

B: Werewolf

C: Zombie

D: Mermaid

30

In which English county is Legoland theme park?

A: Dorset

B: Hertfordshire

C: Berkshire

D: Norfolk

 50:50 Go to page 251   Go to page 263   ? Answers on page 269

12 ◆ £125,000

31

Which parts of the body would interest a chiropodist?

- A: Feet
- B: Ears
- C: Hands
- D: Teeth

32

Inuit is another name for which people?

- A: Eskimo
- B: Romany
- C: Bedouin
- D: Aborigine

33

Which meat is traditionally accompanied by apple sauce?

- A: Pork
- B: Beef
- C: Turkey
- D: Chicken

34

Which game is played with mallets and hoops?

- A: Bowls
- B: Squash
- C: French cricket
- D: Croquet

35

In which country is Mount Vesuvius?

- A: Italy
- B: Greece
- C: Spain
- D: France

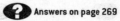50:50 Go to page 251   Go to page 263   ? Answers on page 269

12 ◆ £125,000

36

Which of these fictional characters are not in a set of three?

◆A: Gentlemen of Verona
◆B: Men in a Boat
◆C: Witches in 'Macbeth'
◆D: Wise Men

37

Which of these islands is in the Mediterranean Sea?

◆A: Jamaica
◆B: Crete
◆C: Mauritius
◆D: Guernsey

38

Damon Hill is a former world champion in which sport?

◆A: Athletics
◆B: Snooker
◆C: Motor racing
◆D: Rowing

39

Which of these is a character in 'The Simpsons'?

◆A: Eric Cartman
◆B: Stimpy
◆C: Bender
◆D: Smithers

40

In which month is St David's Day?

◆A: January
◆B: March
◆C: May
◆D: July

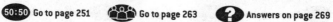

50:50 Go to page 251   Go to page 263   ? Answers on page 269

41

Which member of the Royal Family has children called Peter and Zara?

A: Princess Anne

B: Princess Alexandra

C: Princess Margaret

D: Duchess of Kent

42

Bill Clinton took over from which US president?

A: Jimmy Carter

B: Ronald Reagan

C: George Bush

D: Gerald Ford

43

Peru is a country in which continent?

A: Asia

B: Europe

C: South America

D: Africa

44

Which of these people is famous for writing novels?

A: Thomas Hardy

B: Christopher Wren

C: Louis Pasteur

D: Isaac Newton

50:50 Go to page 251   Go to page 263   ? Answers on page 269

15   £1 MILLION

14   £500,000

13 ◆ £250,000

12 ◆ £125,000

11 ◆ £64,000

10 ◆ £32,000

9 ◆ £16,000

8 ◆ £8,000

7 ◆ £4,000

6 ◆ £2,000

5 ◆ £1,000

4 ◆ £500

3 ◆ £300

2 ◆ £200

1 ◆ £100

13 ◆ £250,000

1

Ochre is a dark shade of which colour?

A: Blue

B: Pink

C: Yellow

D: Purple

2

Which planet orbits the sun approximately every 165 years?

A: Mars

B: Saturn

C: Venus

D: Neptune

3

Which of these is not a position in a standard netball team?

A: Goal centre

B: Goal attack

C: Goalkeeper

D: Goal defence

4

Which of these is a Jewish ceremony traditionally undertaken when a boy reaches the age of 13?

A: Bar Mitzvah

B: Yom Kippur

C: Sukkoth

D: Purim

5

What type of weapon is a blunderbuss?

A: Gun

B: Cannon

C: Sword

D: Arrow

50:50 Go to page 251   Go to page 263   ? Answers on page 269

13 ◆ £250,000

6

Which of these is often a member of a rowing team?

A: Bramley
B: Pippin
C: Cox
D: Braeburn

7

A 'tsunami' is a type of large...what?

A: Dog
B: Wave
C: Hat
D: Country

8

What type of animal is a bat?

A: Reptile
B: Bird
C: Mammal
D: Fish

page
215

9

'Organza' is a type of what?

A: Cheese
B: Fabric
C: Pottery
D: Wine

10

How many signs of the zodiac begin with a vowel?

A: One
B: Two
C: Three
D: Four

50:50 Go to page 251   Go to page 263   ? Answers on page 269

13 ◆ £250,000

11

Dean Macey is a rising star in which athletics event?

- A: Shot put
- B: Hammer
- C: Marathon
- D: Decathlon

12

Which of these is a section of England's east coast between Norfolk and Lincolnshire?

- A: The Wash
- B: The Spin
- C: The Tumble
- D: The Rinse

13

What is a 'chanterelle'?

- A: Slow dance
- B: Breed of antelope
- C: Type of mushroom
- D: Musical instrument

14

Jenson Button drove for which Formula 1 team in his debut season in the sport?

- A: McLaren
- B: Williams
- C: Benetton
- D: Ferrari

15

What type of tower are you said to live in if you are protected from things in everyday life?

- A: Pearl
- B: Ivory
- C: Satin
- D: Water

50:50 Go to page 251   Go to page 263   ? Answers on page 269

13 ◆ £250,000

16

Which musical features the song 'Memory'?

- A: Chess
- B: Annie
- C: Evita
- D: Cats

17

What type of creature is a 'lamprey'?

- A: Fish
- B: Insect
- C: Bird
- D: Deer

18

Which of these is not a country in South America?

- A: Benin
- B: Guyana
- C: Chile
- D: Bolivia

19

What does a 'postilion' ride?

- A: Motorcycle
- B: Penny-farthing
- C: Stagecoach
- D: Horse

20

In which century was Sir Francis Drake born?

- A: 14th
- B: 15th
- C: 16th
- D: 17th

50:50 Go to page 251   Go to page 263   **?** Answers on page 269

13 ◆ £250,000

21

What type of food is 'pak choi'?

A: Vegetable | B: Cheese
C: Bread | D: Fish

22

The 'cranium' is the medical term for which part of the body?

A: Skull | B: Breastbone
C: Kneecap | D: Collarbone

23

What is the unit of currency in Switzerland?

A: Franc | B: Mark
C: Pound | D: Escudo

24

Which of these dinosaurs had two rows of bony plates along its back and tail?

A: Stegosaurus | B: Brachiosaurus
C: Diplodocus | D: Tyrannosaurus rex

25

What type of creature is a 'dab'?

A: Bird | B: Reptile
C: Insect | D: Fish

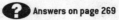
50:50 Go to page 251   Go to page 263   ? Answers on page 269

13 ◆ £250,000

26

Which girl's name is an Aboriginal word for 'boomerang'?

◆A: Karen | ◆B: Kirsty
◆C: Kylie | ◆D: Kerry

27

Jason Queally won an Olympic gold medal in which sport?

◆A: Swimming | ◆B: Athletics
◆C: Cycling | ◆D: Tennis

28

The Lake District is an area of
great natural beauty in which county?

page
219

◆A: Cumbria | ◆B: Essex
◆C: Cornwall | ◆D: Kent

29

What is 'chowder'?

◆A: Waterproof paint | ◆B: Striped fabric
◆C: Plant fertiliser | ◆D: Thick soup

30

By which name is the Dickens character
Jack Dawkins popularly known?

◆A: The Artful Dodger | ◆B: Our Mutual Friend
◆C: Oliver Twist | ◆D: Mr Micawber

 50:50 Go to page 251   Go to page 263   ? Answers on page 269

31

'Muscovy' is which type of creature?

- A: Flatfish
- B: Duck
- C: Monkey
- D: Rodent

32

What is measured with an 'altimeter'?

- A: Pressure
- B: Height
- C: Wind speed
- D: Temperature

33

Which of these books was written by Arthur Ransome?

- A: Tarka the Otter
- B: Black Beauty
- C: White Fang
- D: Swallows and Amazons

34

What is the traditional flavour of a macaroon?

- A: Orange
- B: Peppermint
- C: Chocolate
- D: Almond

35

Which of these is not a French cheese?

- A: Camembert
- B: Brie
- C: Roquefort
- D: Emmental

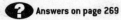
50:50 Go to page 251   Go to page 263   ? Answers on page 269

13 ◆ £250,000

36

To which of these pop groups did singer Sting belong?

- A: Ultravox
- B: Boomtown Rats
- C: Police
- D: Genesis

37

On which island is the volcano Mount Etna?

- A: Sicily
- B: Corsica
- C: Sardinia
- D: Crete

38

The government department responsible for collecting VAT is called 'Customs and...' what?

- A: Excellence
- B: Exchange
- C: Exclusion
- D: Excise

39

Sammy Sosa is a leading figure in which American sport?

- A: Ice hockey
- B: American football
- C: Basketball
- D: Baseball

40

Kuala Lumpur is the capital of which country?

- A: Thailand
- B: Vietnam
- C: Cambodia
- D: Malaysia

50:50 Go to page 251   Go to page 263   ? Answers on page 269

50:50		

15		£1 MILLION
14	◆	**£500,000**
13	◆	£250,000
12	◆	£125,000
11	◆	£64,000
10	◆	**£32,000**
9	◆	£16,000
8	◆	£8,000
7	◆	£4,000
6	◆	£2,000
5	◆	**£1,000**
4	◆	£500
3	◆	£300
2	◆	£200
1	◆	£100

1

In which country did the 'mazurka' dance originate?

- A: Poland
- B: Turkey
- C: Greece
- D: Spain

2

What type of animal is the grey Lipizzaner?

- A: Dog
- B: Horse
- C: Sheep
- D: Cow

3

Who came to the throne when Queen Victoria died?

- A: William IV
- B: Edward VII
- C: George V
- D: George VI

4

Which of these is a type of Asian sailing vessel?

- A: Litter
- B: Trash
- C: Junk
- D: Garbage

5

The Beatles pop group originated in which British city?

- A: Liverpool
- B: Cardiff
- C: Glasgow
- D: Belfast

50:50 Go to page 252   Go to page 264   ? Answers on page 270

14 ◆ £500,000

6

'Mahogany' is a reddish-brown variety of what?

- A: Dog
- B: Tree
- C: Rock
- D: Cloud

7

The disease malaria is usually caused by the bite of which creature?

- A: Cockroach
- B: Spider
- C: Mosquito
- D: Ant

8

page **225**

Which planet is also the name of a poisonous, silvery metallic element?

- A: Saturn
- B: Jupiter
- C: Mars
- D: Mercury

9

Seoul is the capital of which country?

- A: South Korea
- B: Greece
- C: Mexico
- D: Canada

10

Which of these is a tool with a large curved blade, used for cutting grass or crops?

- A: Blithe
- B: Hythe
- C: Writhe
- D: Scythe

50:50 Go to page 252 Go to page 264 **?** Answers on page 270

14 ◆ £500,000

11

Admiral Nelson died on board which ship?

- A: HMS Triumph
- B: HMS Glory
- C: HMS Victory
- D: HMS Endeavour

12

Which of these is a system specifically used for locating objects underwater?

- A: Radar
- B: Sonar
- C: Telegraphy
- D: Semaphore

13

What type of musical instrument are 'timpani'?

- A: Pianos
- B: Saxophones
- C: Drums
- D: Violas

14

Which sport is traditionally played on a 'diamond'?

- A: Baseball
- B: Ice hockey
- C: American football
- D: Basketball

15

Hanukkah is a festival in which religion?

- A: Christianity
- B: Judaism
- C: Hinduism
- D: Buddhism

50:50 Go to page 252   Go to page 264   **?** Answers on page 270

14 ◆ £500,000

16

Which Italian city is built on a lagoon in the Adriatic Sea?

A: Milan

B: Naples

C: Turin

D: Venice

17

Which famous general led elephants across the Alps to attack the Roman Empire?

A: Julius Caesar

B: Hannibal

C: Alexander the Great

D: Genghis Khan

18

In which century was William Shakespeare born?

A: 16th

B: 17th

C: 18th

D: 19th

19

What type of creature is a 'saluki'?

A: Dog

B: Deer

C: Dragonfly

D: Dolphin

20

The French brothers André and Edouard Michelin are most associated with the manufacture of what?

A: Tyres

B: Saucepans

C: Pianos

D: Watches

50:50 Go to page 252   Go to page 264   Answers on page 270

21

In the human body, what is another term for the 'scapula'?

A: Thighbone
B: Breastbone
C: Kneecap
D: Shoulder blade

22

Which of these words means the formal resignation of a king or queen?

A: Aberration
B: Ablation
C: Absolution
D: Abdication

23

Which of these is one of the Channel Islands?

A: Yell
B: Sark
C: Hoy
D: Anglesey

24

In the New Testament, who was the first person to see Jesus after his resurrection?

A: Mary Modena
B: Mary Matilda
C: Mary Magdalene
D: Mary Martha

25

Which of these resorts boasts the longest seaside pier?

A: Blackpool
B: Skegness
C: Brighton
D: Southend

50:50 Go to page 252   Go to page 264   ? Answers on page 270

14 ◆ £500,000

26

What was the title of the album released by Martine McCutcheon in 2000?

A: Wishing | B: Hoping
C: Loving | D: Praying

27

In T.S. Eliot's 'Old Possum's Book of Practical Cats', what is the name of the Railway Cat?

A: Macavity | B: Griddlebone
C: Skimbleshanks | D: Bustopher Jones

28

In which country is Lake Eyre?

A: Canada | B: Australia
C: South Africa | D: Scotland

29

The Babington Plot of 1586 was a conspiracy to kill which monarch?

A: Charles II | B: Henry VIII
C: Victoria | D: Elizabeth I

30

Aylesbury is the county town of which county?

A: Hertfordshire | B: Bedfordshire
C: Northamptonshire | D: Buckinghamshire

14 ◆ £500,000

31

On which planet is the volcano Olympus Mons?

A: Jupiter
B: Saturn
C: Venus
D: Mars

32

On which farm does Worzel Gummidge live
in the books by Barbara Euphan Todd?

A: Meadow Farm
B: Steppingstone Farm
C: Oak Apple Farm
D: Scatterbrook Farm

33

Who claimed to have 'the heart and stomach of a king'?

A: Elizabeth I
B: Victoria
C: Florence Nightingale
D: Cleopatra

34

In which city is the Brandenburg Gate?

A: Berlin
B: Budapest
C: Bonn
D: Bergen

35

Who was on the British throne at
the outbreak of World War II?

A: George V
B: Edward VIII
C: George VI
D: Elizabeth II

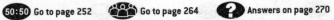

50:50 Go to page 252   Go to page 264   ? Answers on page 270

36

In which century was the French Revolution?

A: 16th

B: 17th

C: 18th

D: 19th

50:50 Go to page 252   Go to page 264   Answers on page 270

15 ◆ £1 MILLION

14 ◆ £500,000

13 ◆ £250,000

12 ◆ £125,000

11 ◆ £64,000

10 ◆ £32,000

9 ◆ £16,000

8 ◆ £8,000

7 ◆ £4,000

6 ◆ £2,000

5 ◆ £1,000

4 ◆ £500

3 ◆ £300

2 ◆ £200

1 ◆ £100

15 ◆ £1,000,000

1

Shinto is the most popular religion in which of these countries?

- A: China
- B: Thailand
- C: Japan
- D: India

2

The 'femur' is a bone in which part of the human body?

- A: Arm
- B: Head
- C: Leg
- D: Hand

3

What is the name of a pattern or picture made up of small pieces of coloured stone or glass?

- A: Mosaic
- B: Icon
- C: Triptych
- D: Miniature

4

What chemical makes up about four-fifths of the Earth's air?

- A: Hydrogen
- B: Oxygen
- C: Nitrogen
- D: Argon

5

The faces of which people have been carved on Mount Rushmore in the USA?

- A: Presidents
- B: Musicians
- C: Sportsmen
- D: Film stars

50:50 Go to page 252   Go to page 264   ? Answers on page 270

15 ◆ £1,000,000

6

What is the medical name for the part of the human body known as the 'windpipe'?

- A: Trachea
- B: Spleen
- C: Humerus
- D: Fibula

7

Which US city is known as 'the Windy City'?

- A: New York
- B: Los Angeles
- C: Chicago
- D: Florida

8

Which type of animal lives in a sett?

- A: Badger
- B: Fox
- C: Beaver
- D: Stoat

9

Prince Rainier III is the head of state of which principality?

- A: Monaco
- B: Mongolia
- C: Mombasa
- D: Montenegro

10

What does a 'barometer' measure?

- A: Atmospheric pressure
- B: Radiation
- C: Seismic activity
- D: Wind speed

50:50 Go to page 252   Go to page 264   ? Answers on page 270

15 ◆ £1,000,000

11

Which of these islands is not in the Caribbean Sea?

- A: Sardinia
- B: Martinique
- C: Grenada
- D: Antigua

12

What was the first name of the Victorian prime minister Disraeli?

- A: William
- B: Benjamin
- C: Harold
- D: Robert

13

Which type of animal lives in an 'eyrie'?

- A: Eagle
- B: Otter
- C: Weasel
- D: Bear

14

Which of these is the common pattern on gingham fabric?

- A: Checks
- B: Spots
- C: Flowers
- D: Swirls

15

Which style of painting is most associated with the artist Claude Monet?

- A: Impressionism
- B: Pointillism
- C: Surrealism
- D: Cubism

50:50 Go to page 252   Go to page 264   ? Answers on page 270

15 ◆ £1,000,000

16

In which African country is the area of Mashonaland?

- A: Kenya
- B: Egypt
- C: Mozambique
- D: Zimbabwe

17

In the periodic table, what is another name for the inert gases?

- A: Virtuous
- B: Brave
- C: Noble
- D: Dignified

18

Under which landmark in Paris is the grave of France's 'Unknown Soldier'?

- A: Arc de Triomphe
- B: Eiffel Tower
- C: Louvre
- D: Notre Dame Cathedral

19

'The Blue Boy' is a famous painting by which artist?

- A: Claude Monet
- B: John Constable
- C: Leonardo da Vinci
- D: Thomas Gainsborough

20

What is the capital of the US state of Minnesota?

- A: St Peter
- B: St John
- C: St Paul
- D: St James

50:50 Go to page 252   Go to page 264   ? Answers on page 270

15 ◆ £1,000,000

21

Which birds belong to the order Strigiformes?

- A: Eagles
- B: Owls
- C: Geese
- D: Pigeons

22

'Rutabaga' is an American term for which vegetable?

- A: Swede
- B: Carrot
- C: Parsnip
- D: Courgette

23

In Greek mythology, who killed the Minotaur?

- A: Daedalus
- B: Dionysus
- C: Perseus
- D: Theseus

24

What was the first name of Ferrari, the Italian racing car designer?

- A: Enrico
- B: Enzo
- C: Roberto
- D: Luciano

25

In old money, how many shillings were equal to one guinea?

- A: 18
- B: 20
- C: 21
- D: 24

50:50 Go to page 252   Go to page 264   ? Answers on page 270

15 ◆ £1,000,000

26

Which of these posts was held by Donald Coggan?

A: Archbishop of Canterbury
B: Poet Laureate
C: US President
D: UK Prime Minister

27

Shiva is an important deity in which religion?

A: Judaism
B: Shintoism
C: Hinduism
D: Christianity

28

What was the first name of Shakespeare's mother?

A: Mary
B: Anne
C: Elizabeth
D: Susan

29

In which English county is Winston Churchill's birthplace, Blenheim Palace?

A: Buckinghamshire
B: Bedfordshire
C: Hertfordshire
D: Oxfordshire

30

Which US state is known as the Bluegrass State?

A: Idaho
B: Kentucky
C: California
D: Texas

50:50 Go to page 252   Go to page 264   Answers on page 270

31

In the periodic table, what is the atomic number of oxygen?

A: 1

B: 2

C: 8

D: 12

32

Which Russian tsar was married to Alexandra?

A: Nicholas

B: Ivan

C: Peter

D: Alexander

50:50

£100

1	Options remaining are A and C	38	Options remaining are B and C
2	Options remaining are B and D	39	Options remaining are A and D
3	Options remaining are B and D	40	Options remaining are A and C
4	Options remaining are C and D	41	Options remaining are A and D
5	Options remaining are A and D	42	Options remaining are A and D
6	Options remaining are B and C	43	Options remaining are A and D
7	Options remaining are B and D	44	Options remaining are A and B
8	Options remaining are A and B	45	Options remaining are C and D
9	Options remaining are A and C	46	Options remaining are A and C
10	Options remaining are A and D	47	Options remaining are C and D
11	Options remaining are B and D	48	Options remaining are A and D
12	Options remaining are A and B	49	Options remaining are A and D
13	Options remaining are A and B	50	Options remaining are A and D
14	Options remaining are A and B	51	Options remaining are A and D
15	Options remaining are B and C	52	Options remaining are B and C
16	Options remaining are A and D	53	Options remaining are C and D
17	Options remaining are B and C	54	Options remaining are A and D
18	Options remaining are A and B	55	Options remaining are A and D
19	Options remaining are A and D	56	Options remaining are A and D
20	Options remaining are B and C	57	Options remaining are C and D
21	Options remaining are C and D	58	Options remaining are A and B
22	Options remaining are C and D	59	Options remaining are A and C
23	Options remaining are C and D	60	Options remaining are A and C
24	Options remaining are B and C	61	Options remaining are A and B
25	Options remaining are A and B	62	Options remaining are A and D
26	Options remaining are A and B	63	Options remaining are A and C
27	Options remaining are A and B	64	Options remaining are B and D
28	Options remaining are A and C	65	Options remaining are A and D
29	Options remaining are B and C	66	Options remaining are A and B
30	Options remaining are A and B	67	Options remaining are A and D
31	Options remaining are A and D	68	Options remaining are A and D
32	Options remaining are A and C	69	Options remaining are A and C
33	Options remaining are A and D	70	Options remaining are A and D
34	Options remaining are A and D	71	Options remaining are B and D
35	Options remaining are B and D	72	Options remaining are A and B
36	Options remaining are A and D	73	Options remaining are A and C
37	Options remaining are A and C	74	Options remaining are A and C

50:50

75	Options remaining are A and B	82	Options remaining are A and C
76	Options remaining are A and D	83	Options remaining are B and C
77	Options remaining are A and B	84	Options remaining are A and D
78	Options remaining are A and C	85	Options remaining are A and C
79	Options remaining are A and C	86	Options remaining are A and D
80	Options remaining are A and C	87	Options remaining are A and D
81	Options remaining are A and C	88	Options remaining are A and C

£200

1	Options remaining are B and D	33	Options remaining are A and B
2	Options remaining are A and D	34	Options remaining are A and D
3	Options remaining are A and D	35	Options remaining are A and C
4	Options remaining are C and D	36	Options remaining are C and D
5	Options remaining are A and B	37	Options remaining are A and D
6	Options remaining are A and D	38	Options remaining are A and D
7	Options remaining are A and D	39	Options remaining are A and D
8	Options remaining are A and D	40	Options remaining are A and D
9	Options remaining are A and C	41	Options remaining are A and B
10	Options remaining are A and D	42	Options remaining are A and B
11	Options remaining are A and C	43	Options remaining are A and D
12	Options remaining are A and C	44	Options remaining are B and C
13	Options remaining are A and C	45	Options remaining are B and C
14	Options remaining are A and D	46	Options remaining are A and B
15	Options remaining are A and D	47	Options remaining are C and D
16	Options remaining are A and C	48	Options remaining are A and C
17	Options remaining are C and D	49	Options remaining are A and C
18	Options remaining are B and D	50	Options remaining are B and D
19	Options remaining are A and D	51	Options remaining are A and B
20	Options remaining are A and B	52	Options remaining are A and B
21	Options remaining are A and C	53	Options remaining are C and D
22	Options remaining are A and D	54	Options remaining are A and B
23	Options remaining are A and D	55	Options remaining are B and C
24	Options remaining are C and D	56	Options remaining are C and D
25	Options remaining are B and C	57	Options remaining are A and C
26	Options remaining are A and D	58	Options remaining are B and D
27	Options remaining are A and C	59	Options remaining are B and C
28	Options remaining are B and C	60	Options remaining are A and D
29	Options remaining are C and D	61	Options remaining are C and D
30	Options remaining are A and C	62	Options remaining are A and D
31	Options remaining are A and C	63	Options remaining are A and B
32	Options remaining are A and B	64	Options remaining are A and B

50:50

65	Options remaining are A and C	75	Options remaining are A and D
66	Options remaining are C and D	76	Options remaining are B and C
67	Options remaining are A and D	77	Options remaining are A and C
68	Options remaining are A and C	78	Options remaining are A and D
69	Options remaining are A and B	79	Options remaining are A and D
70	Options remaining are A and D	80	Options remaining are A and C
71	Options remaining are A and B	81	Options remaining are A and C
72	Options remaining are A and B	82	Options remaining are B and D
73	Options remaining are A and B	83	Options remaining are B and D
74	Options remaining are A and C	84	Options remaining are A and D

£300

1	Options remaining are A and D	30	Options remaining are B and D
2	Options remaining are A and D	31	Options remaining are C and D
3	Options remaining are A and D	32	Options remaining are C and D
4	Options remaining are A and D	33	Options remaining are C and D
5	Options remaining are B and D	34	Options remaining are A and D
6	Options remaining are A and C	35	Options remaining are A and C
7	Options remaining are A and D	36	Options remaining are C and D
8	Options remaining are A and B	37	Options remaining are A and B
9	Options remaining are A and B	38	Options remaining are A and B
10	Options remaining are B and D	39	Options remaining are B and D
11	Options remaining are A and B	40	Options remaining are C and D
12	Options remaining are B and D	41	Options remaining are A and D
13	Options remaining are B and D	42	Options remaining are A and C
14	Options remaining are C and D	43	Options remaining are B and C
15	Options remaining are A and C	44	Options remaining are B and C
16	Options remaining are A and C	45	Options remaining are B and D
17	Options remaining are A and B	46	Options remaining are A and C
18	Options remaining are A and B	47	Options remaining are A and B
19	Options remaining are C and D	48	Options remaining are A and D
20	Options remaining are A and D	49	Options remaining are A and B
21	Options remaining are C and D	50	Options remaining are B and C
22	Options remaining are C and D	51	Options remaining are A and D
23	Options remaining are C and D	52	Options remaining are A and C
24	Options remaining are A and B	53	Options remaining are A and C
25	Options remaining are A and B	54	Options remaining are C and D
26	Options remaining are A and D	55	Options remaining are C and D
27	Options remaining are A and D	56	Options remaining are A and D
28	Options remaining are A and B	57	Options remaining are A and C
29	Options remaining are A and C	58	Options remaining are B and D

50:50

59	Options remaining are A and D	70	Options remaining are A and C
60	Options remaining are B and D	71	Options remaining are A and D
61	Options remaining are A and C	72	Options remaining are B and D
62	Options remaining are A and B	73	Options remaining are A and B
63	Options remaining are A and B	74	Options remaining are C and D
64	Options remaining are A and C	75	Options remaining are A and B
65	Options remaining are A and C	76	Options remaining are A and B
66	Options remaining are C and D	77	Options remaining are A and D
67	Options remaining are A and C	78	Options remaining are B and C
68	Options remaining are A and C	79	Options remaining are B and D
69	Options remaining are A and C	80	Options remaining are A and D

£500

1	Options remaining are B and D	29	Options remaining are C and D
2	Options remaining are A and B	30	Options remaining are B and D
3	Options remaining are B and C	31	Options remaining are B and D
4	Options remaining are A and D	32	Options remaining are A and C
5	Options remaining are A and D	33	Options remaining are A and B
6	Options remaining are A and D	34	Options remaining are A and D
7	Options remaining are A and C	35	Options remaining are B and C
8	Options remaining are A and C	36	Options remaining are B and D
9	Options remaining are A and C	37	Options remaining are A and C
10	Options remaining are A and D	38	Options remaining are A and C
11	Options remaining are A and B	39	Options remaining are B and D
12	Options remaining are A and C	40	Options remaining are B and C
13	Options remaining are A and C	41	Options remaining are A and D
14	Options remaining are A and D	42	Options remaining are C and D
15	Options remaining are C and D	43	Options remaining are B and C
16	Options remaining are A and C	44	Options remaining are B and C
17	Options remaining are A and C	45	Options remaining are B and D
18	Options remaining are A and D	46	Options remaining are A and D
19	Options remaining are A and B	47	Options remaining are A and C
20	Options remaining are A and C	48	Options remaining are B and D
21	Options remaining are A and C	49	Options remaining are A and C
22	Options remaining are B and C	50	Options remaining are A and B
23	Options remaining are A and D	51	Options remaining are A and C
24	Options remaining are A and D	52	Options remaining are C and D
25	Options remaining are B and C	53	Options remaining are B and D
26	Options remaining are B and D	54	Options remaining are C and D
27	Options remaining are B and D	55	Options remaining are B and D
28	Options remaining are C and D	56	Options remaining are A and B

50:50

57 Options remaining are B and C	67 Options remaining are A and C
58 Options remaining are A and C	68 Options remaining are B and D
59 Options remaining are A and C	69 Options remaining are B and C
60 Options remaining are B and D	70 Options remaining are B and D
61 Options remaining are A and D	71 Options remaining are A and C
62 Options remaining are A and D	72 Options remaining are A and C
63 Options remaining are B and C	73 Options remaining are B and C
64 Options remaining are A and C	74 Options remaining are A and D
65 Options remaining are A and D	75 Options remaining are B and C
66 Options remaining are A and D	76 Options remaining are B and C

£1,000

1 Options remaining are A and D	30 Options remaining are A and C
2 Options remaining are B and C	31 Options remaining are B and D
3 Options remaining are A and B	32 Options remaining are A and D
4 Options remaining are B and D	33 Options remaining are B and C
5 Options remaining are A and C	34 Options remaining are A and B
6 Options remaining are B and D	35 Options remaining are A and B
7 Options remaining are A and C	36 Options remaining are C and D
8 Options remaining are A and C	37 Options remaining are C and D
9 Options remaining are B and C	38 Options remaining are B and D
10 Options remaining are A and C	39 Options remaining are B and C
11 Options remaining are A and D	40 Options remaining are A and D
12 Options remaining are A and C	41 Options remaining are C and D
13 Options remaining are A and D	42 Options remaining are B and C
14 Options remaining are A and C	43 Options remaining are B and C
15 Options remaining are A and D	44 Options remaining are B and D
16 Options remaining are B and D	45 Options remaining are C and D
17 Options remaining are A and D	46 Options remaining are B and D
18 Options remaining are A and D	47 Options remaining are B and D
19 Options remaining are A and D	48 Options remaining are A and B
20 Options remaining are A and C	49 Options remaining are A and B
21 Options remaining are A and C	50 Options remaining are C and D
22 Options remaining are A and C	51 Options remaining are B and C
23 Options remaining are A and B	52 Options remaining are B and C
24 Options remaining are A and B	53 Options remaining are A and C
25 Options remaining are A and D	54 Options remaining are C and D
26 Options remaining are A and C	55 Options remaining are A and D
27 Options remaining are A and B	56 Options remaining are A and D
28 Options remaining are C and D	57 Options remaining are A and D
29 Options remaining are C and D	58 Options remaining are B and C

59 Options remaining are C and D
60 Options remaining are A and C
61 Options remaining are A and C
62 Options remaining are A and B
63 Options remaining are C and D
64 Options remaining are C and D
65 Options remaining are B and D

66 Options remaining are C and D
67 Options remaining are A and D
68 Options remaining are A and D
69 Options remaining are B and D
70 Options remaining are A and D
71 Options remaining are A and B
72 Options remaining are A and D

£2,000

1 Options remaining are A and B
2 Options remaining are A and B
3 Options remaining are A and D
4 Options remaining are A and D
5 Options remaining are C and D
6 Options remaining are B and C
7 Options remaining are A and C
8 Options remaining are A and C
9 Options remaining are A and D
10 Options remaining are A and D
11 Options remaining are A and B
12 Options remaining are C and D
13 Options remaining are A and C
14 Options remaining are B and D
15 Options remaining are A and D
16 Options remaining are B and D
17 Options remaining are A and D
18 Options remaining are A and B
19 Options remaining are C and D
20 Options remaining are A and D
21 Options remaining are A and D
22 Options remaining are B and D
23 Options remaining are B and C
24 Options remaining are B and C
25 Options remaining are A and D
26 Options remaining are A and C
27 Options remaining are A and D
28 Options remaining are A and B
29 Options remaining are B and C
30 Options remaining are C and D
31 Options remaining are C and D

32 Options remaining are A and B
33 Options remaining are A and C
34 Options remaining are A and D
35 Options remaining are A and C
36 Options remaining are A and C
37 Options remaining are C and D
38 Options remaining are A and D
39 Options remaining are B and D
40 Options remaining are B and D
41 Options remaining are B and D
42 Options remaining are A and C
43 Options remaining are A and D
44 Options remaining are B and C
45 Options remaining are A and B
46 Options remaining are A and D
47 Options remaining are C and D
48 Options remaining are C and D
49 Options remaining are B and C
50 Options remaining are B and C
51 Options remaining are A and D
52 Options remaining are A and B
53 Options remaining are A and D
54 Options remaining are B and C
55 Options remaining are A and B
56 Options remaining are B and D
57 Options remaining are A and B
58 Options remaining are B and C
59 Options remaining are C and D
60 Options remaining are B and C
61 Options remaining are A and C
62 Options remaining are A and B

63 Options remaining are B and D	66 Options remaining are B and C
64 Options remaining are A and B	67 Options remaining are C and D
65 Options remaining are A and C	68 Options remaining are A and D

£4,000

1 Options remaining are C and D	33 Options remaining are C and D
2 Options remaining are A and B	34 Options remaining are B and C
3 Options remaining are C and D	35 Options remaining are A and B
4 Options remaining are A and B	36 Options remaining are A and B
5 Options remaining are A and B	37 Options remaining are A and C
6 Options remaining are A and C	38 Options remaining are A and C
7 Options remaining are A and D	39 Options remaining are C and D
8 Options remaining are B and D	40 Options remaining are B and C
9 Options remaining are C and D	41 Options remaining are C and D
10 Options remaining are B and C	42 Options remaining are B and D
11 Options remaining are B and D	43 Options remaining are A and C
12 Options remaining are B and D	44 Options remaining are A and B
13 Options remaining are A and D	45 Options remaining are C and D
14 Options remaining are C and D	46 Options remaining are B and C
15 Options remaining are A and D	47 Options remaining are A and B
16 Options remaining are A and D	48 Options remaining are A and C
17 Options remaining are C and D	49 Options remaining are A and D
18 Options remaining are A and D	50 Options remaining are B and C
19 Options remaining are A and D	51 Options remaining are B and D
20 Options remaining are A and C	52 Options remaining are A and C
21 Options remaining are A and C	53 Options remaining are B and C
22 Options remaining are A and C	54 Options remaining are A and C
23 Options remaining are A and D	55 Options remaining are C and D
24 Options remaining are A and B	56 Options remaining are B and C
25 Options remaining are C and D	57 Options remaining are B and C
26 Options remaining are A and D	58 Options remaining are B and C
27 Options remaining are C and D	59 Options remaining are A and B
28 Options remaining are B and D	60 Options remaining are A and D
29 Options remaining are A and C	61 Options remaining are A and C
30 Options remaining are A and D	62 Options remaining are A and D
31 Options remaining are A and B	63 Options remaining are A and C
32 Options remaining are A and C	64 Options remaining are A and D

50:50

£8,000

1 Options remaining are B and D	31 Options remaining are A and D
2 Options remaining are C and D	32 Options remaining are A and C
3 Options remaining are A and B	33 Options remaining are A and C
4 Options remaining are B and D	34 Options remaining are A and D
5 Options remaining are A and C	35 Options remaining are A and B
6 Options remaining are A and B	36 Options remaining are A and B
7 Options remaining are A and D	37 Options remaining are A and D
8 Options remaining are B and D	38 Options remaining are C and D
9 Options remaining are B and D	39 Options remaining are A and C
10 Options remaining are A and D	40 Options remaining are C and D
11 Options remaining are A and B	41 Options remaining are A and D
12 Options remaining are A and D	42 Options remaining are A and C
13 Options remaining are B and C	43 Options remaining are A and C
14 Options remaining are A and B	44 Options remaining are B and D
15 Options remaining are A and C	45 Options remaining are C and D
16 Options remaining are A and B	46 Options remaining are A and B
17 Options remaining are A and D	47 Options remaining are A and D
18 Options remaining are A and D	48 Options remaining are A and C
19 Options remaining are A and C	49 Options remaining are A and B
20 Options remaining are A and D	50 Options remaining are C and D
21 Options remaining are A and C	51 Options remaining are A and B
22 Options remaining are A and D	52 Options remaining are B and D
23 Options remaining are A and D	53 Options remaining are C and D
24 Options remaining are A and B	54 Options remaining are A and D
25 Options remaining are B and D	55 Options remaining are A and D
26 Options remaining are B and D	56 Options remaining are A and B
27 Options remaining are A and D	57 Options remaining are A and C
28 Options remaining are A and D	58 Options remaining are A and B
29 Options remaining are B and D	59 Options remaining are A and B
30 Options remaining are B and D	60 Options remaining are A and B

£16,000

1 Options remaining are A and D	10 Options remaining are A and B
2 Options remaining are A and C	11 Options remaining are A and B
3 Options remaining are A and D	12 Options remaining are B and C
4 Options remaining are A and C	13 Options remaining are A and B
5 Options remaining are A and B	14 Options remaining are A and C
6 Options remaining are A and D	15 Options remaining are A and D
7 Options remaining are A and C	16 Options remaining are A and C
8 Options remaining are B and D	17 Options remaining are A and C
9 Options remaining are A and C	18 Options remaining are A and C

50:50

19 Options remaining are A and C
20 Options remaining are B and D
21 Options remaining are C and D
22 Options remaining are B and D
23 Options remaining are A and D
24 Options remaining are C and D
25 Options remaining are A and B
26 Options remaining are A and D
27 Options remaining are C and D
28 Options remaining are A and D
29 Options remaining are B and D
30 Options remaining are A and D
31 Options remaining are A and B
32 Options remaining are B and D
33 Options remaining are B and D
34 Options remaining are A and D
35 Options remaining are A and B
36 Options remaining are A and C
37 Options remaining are A and C

38 Options remaining are B and D
39 Options remaining are C and D
40 Options remaining are B and C
41 Options remaining are A and C
42 Options remaining are A and B
43 Options remaining are A and D
44 Options remaining are A and C
45 Options remaining are C and D
46 Options remaining are C and D
47 Options remaining are A and C
48 Options remaining are A and B
49 Options remaining are A and C
50 Options remaining are B and C
51 Options remaining are A and B
52 Options remaining are A and B
53 Options remaining are A and B
54 Options remaining are A and D
55 Options remaining are A and B
56 Options remaining are C and D

£32,000

1   Options remaining are A and B
2   Options remaining are B and D
3   Options remaining are C and D
4   Options remaining are A and C
5   Options remaining are A and B
6   Options remaining are B and C
7   Options remaining are A and D
8   Options remaining are A and B
9   Options remaining are B and C
10 Options remaining are A and D
11 Options remaining are A and C
12 Options remaining are A and B
13 Options remaining are A and D
14 Options remaining are B and D
15 Options remaining are A and D
16 Options remaining are C and D
17 Options remaining are A and C
18 Options remaining are A and D
19 Options remaining are B and D
20 Options remaining are A and C

21 Options remaining are A and D
22 Options remaining are A and D
23 Options remaining are B and C
24 Options remaining are A and C
25 Options remaining are B and D
26 Options remaining are B and C
27 Options remaining are A and B
28 Options remaining are A and B
29 Options remaining are A and C
30 Options remaining are B and C
31 Options remaining are B and C
32 Options remaining are A and D
33 Options remaining are B and C
34 Options remaining are C and D
35 Options remaining are A and C
36 Options remaining are A and C
37 Options remaining are B and D
38 Options remaining are B and C
39 Options remaining are C and D
40 Options remaining are A and D

50:50

41 Options remaining are C and D
42 Options remaining are A and D
43 Options remaining are A and C
44 Options remaining are C and D
45 Options remaining are A and D
46 Options remaining are A and D

47 Options remaining are A and C
48 Options remaining are B and C
49 Options remaining are A and B
50 Options remaining are A and D
51 Options remaining are C and D
52 Options remaining are A and C

£64,000

1   Options remaining are C and D
2   Options remaining are A and C
3   Options remaining are C and D
4   Options remaining are A and C
5   Options remaining are A and C
6   Options remaining are A and C
7   Options remaining are B and D
8   Options remaining are A and D
9   Options remaining are B and D
10 Options remaining are A and C
11 Options remaining are A and D
12 Options remaining are A and D
13 Options remaining are A and C
14 Options remaining are B and C
15 Options remaining are B and D
16 Options remaining are A and D
17 Options remaining are A and B
18 Options remaining are A and C
19 Options remaining are B and C
20 Options remaining are A and D
21 Options remaining are A and B
22 Options remaining are B and C
23 Options remaining are B and C
24 Options remaining are A and C

25 Options remaining are A and D
26 Options remaining are A and B
27 Options remaining are B and D
28 Options remaining are B and D
29 Options remaining are A and D
30 Options remaining are A and D
31 Options remaining are A and C
32 Options remaining are A and B
33 Options remaining are A and D
34 Options remaining are B and C
35 Options remaining are B and C
36 Options remaining are A and C
37 Options remaining are A and D
38 Options remaining are B and D
39 Options remaining are A and D
40 Options remaining are A and D
41 Options remaining are A and D
42 Options remaining are A and C
43 Options remaining are B and C
44 Options remaining are C and D
45 Options remaining are B and C
46 Options remaining are B and D
47 Options remaining are C and D
48 Options remaining are A and D

£125,000

1   Options remaining are A and D
2   Options remaining are A and D
3   Options remaining are B and D
4   Options remaining are A and B
5   Options remaining are A and D

6   Options remaining are C and D
7   Options remaining are A and D
8   Options remaining are C and D
9   Options remaining are C and D
10 Options remaining are B and D

50:50

11	Options remaining are A and C	28	Options remaining are A and B
12	Options remaining are B and D	29	Options remaining are A and B
13	Options remaining are A and B	30	Options remaining are C and D
14	Options remaining are A and D	31	Options remaining are A and B
15	Options remaining are A and C	32	Options remaining are A and D
16	Options remaining are A and D	33	Options remaining are A and B
17	Options remaining are A and D	34	Options remaining are C and D
18	Options remaining are B and C	35	Options remaining are A and B
19	Options remaining are A and B	36	Options remaining are A and B
20	Options remaining are A and D	37	Options remaining are A and B
21	Options remaining are B and D	38	Options remaining are A and C
22	Options remaining are A and C	39	Options remaining are A and D
23	Options remaining are B and D	40	Options remaining are B and D
24	Options remaining are C and D	41	Options remaining are A and B
25	Options remaining are B and D	42	Options remaining are B and C
26	Options remaining are B and D	43	Options remaining are A and C
27	Options remaining are A and D	44	Options remaining are A and D

£250,000

1	Options remaining are C and D	21	Options remaining are A and C
2	Options remaining are B and D	22	Options remaining are A and C
3	Options remaining are A and B	23	Options remaining are A and B
4	Options remaining are A and D	24	Options remaining are A and B
5	Options remaining are A and D	25	Options remaining are A and D
6	Options remaining are A and C	26	Options remaining are C and D
7	Options remaining are A and B	27	Options remaining are A and C
8	Options remaining are A and C	28	Options remaining are A and D
9	Options remaining are B and C	29	Options remaining are A and D
10	Options remaining are B and C	30	Options remaining are A and B
11	Options remaining are A and D	31	Options remaining are B and D
12	Options remaining are A and D	32	Options remaining are B and C
13	Options remaining are B and C	33	Options remaining are C and D
14	Options remaining are A and B	34	Options remaining are B and D
15	Options remaining are B and C	35	Options remaining are A and D
16	Options remaining are A and D	36	Options remaining are C and D
17	Options remaining are A and B	37	Options remaining are A and B
18	Options remaining are A and B	38	Options remaining are B and D
19	Options remaining are A and D	39	Options remaining are A and D
20	Options remaining are B and C	40	Options remaining are A and D

50:50

£500,000

1	Options remaining are A and C	19	Options remaining are A and B
2	Options remaining are B and D	20	Options remaining are A and C
3	Options remaining are B and C	21	Options remaining are C and D
4	Options remaining are A and C	22	Options remaining are A and D
5	Options remaining are A and C	23	Options remaining are A and B
6	Options remaining are B and D	24	Options remaining are C and D
7	Options remaining are A and C	25	Options remaining are C and D
8	Options remaining are A and D	26	Options remaining are A and D
9	Options remaining are A and D	27	Options remaining are C and D
10	Options remaining are C and D	28	Options remaining are A and B
11	Options remaining are A and C	29	Options remaining are A and D
12	Options remaining are B and D	30	Options remaining are B and D
13	Options remaining are C and D	31	Options remaining are A and D
14	Options remaining are A and D	32	Options remaining are A and D
15	Options remaining are B and D	33	Options remaining are A and D
16	Options remaining are C and D	34	Options remaining are A and C
17	Options remaining are B and D	35	Options remaining are C and D
18	Options remaining are A and B	36	Options remaining are B and C

£1,000,000

1	Options remaining are A and C	17	Options remaining are A and C
2	Options remaining are A and C	18	Options remaining are A and B
3	Options remaining are A and D	19	Options remaining are B and D
4	Options remaining are A and C	20	Options remaining are A and C
5	Options remaining are A and D	21	Options remaining are B and C
6	Options remaining are A and D	22	Options remaining are A and C
7	Options remaining are A and C	23	Options remaining are C and D
8	Options remaining are A and D	24	Options remaining are A and B
9	Options remaining are A and D	25	Options remaining are C and D
10	Options remaining are A and D	26	Options remaining are A and B
11	Options remaining are A and D	27	Options remaining are A and C
12	Options remaining are A and B	28	Options remaining are A and B
13	Options remaining are A and C	29	Options remaining are B and D
14	Options remaining are A and D	30	Options remaining are A and B
15	Options remaining are A and C	31	Options remaining are B and C
16	Options remaining are A and D	32	Options remaining are A and C

Ask The Audience

£100

#	A	B	C	D
1	A:0%	B:0%	C:100%	D:0%
2	A:10%	B:16%	C:0%	D:74%
3	A:0%	B:0%	C:0%	D:100%
4	A:0%	B:0%	C:0%	D:100%
5	A:89%	B:0%	C:0%	D:11%
6	A:0%	B:89%	C:11%	D:0%
7	A:0%	B:100%	C:0%	D:0%
8	A:0%	B:100%	C:0%	D:0%
9	A:0%	B:0%	C:100%	D:0%
10	A:5%	B:0%	C:0%	D:95%
11	A:0%	B:100%	C:0%	D:0%
12	A:0%	B:100%	C:0%	D:0%
13	A:0%	B:100%	C:0%	D:0%
14	A:95%	B:0%	C:5%	D:0%
15	A:5%	B:0%	C:95%	D:0%
16	A:100%	B:0%	C:0%	D:0%
17	A:0%	B:0%	C:100%	D:0%
18	A:100%	B:0%	C:0%	D:0%
19	A:8%	B:0%	C:5%	D:87%
20	A:0%	B:74%	C:0%	D:26%
21	A:0%	B:0%	C:100%	D:0%
22	A:5%	B:6%	C:89%	D:0%
23	A:37%	B:0%	C:5%	D:58%
24	A:6%	B:26%	C:68%	D:0%
25	A:0%	B:95%	C:5%	D:0%
26	A:5%	B:88%	C:7%	D:0%
27	A:0%	B:100%	C:0%	D:0%
28	A:100%	B:0%	C:0%	D:0%
29	A:0%	B:95%	C:0%	D:5%
30	A:0%	B:100%	C:0%	D:0%
31	A:0%	B:12%	C:0%	D:88%
32	A:89%	B:6%	C:5%	D:0%
33	A:100%	B:0%	C:0%	D:0%
34	A:0%	B:0%	C:0%	D:100%
35	A:0%	B:100%	C:0%	D:0%
36	A:0%	B:5%	C:0%	D:95%
37	A:95%	B:0%	C:5%	D:0%
38	A:6%	B:0%	C:89%	D:5%
39	A:0%	B:0%	C:0%	D:100%
40	A:0%	B:0%	C:100%	D:0%
41	A:79%	B:0%	C:11%	D:10%
42	A:0%	B:5%	C:0%	D:95%
43	A:0%	B:0%	C:0%	D:100%
44	A:26%	B:74%	C:0%	D:0%
45	A:5%	B:5%	C:79%	D:11%
46	A:0%	B:0%	C:100%	D:0%
47	A:0%	B:0%	C:100%	D:0%
48	A:0%	B:12%	C:0%	D:88%
49	A:100%	B:0%	C:0%	D:0%
50	A:5%	B:0%	C:0%	D:95%
51	A:0%	B:0%	C:16%	D:84%
52	A:6%	B:10%	C:84%	D:0%
53	A:0%	B:0%	C:0%	D:100%
54	A:0%	B:5%	C:16%	D:79%
55	A:0%	B:6%	C:5%	D:89%
56	A:63%	B:11%	C:0%	D:26%
57	A:0%	B:0%	C:5%	D:95%
58	A:0%	B:89%	C:11%	D:0%
59	A:0%	B:0%	C:95%	D:5%
60	A:0%	B:0%	C:94%	D:6%
61	A:42%	B:53%	C:0%	D:5%
62	A:100%	B:0%	C:0%	D:0%
63	A:100%	B:0%	C:0%	D:0%
64	A:0%	B:100%	C:0%	D:0%
65	A:74%	B:5%	C:5%	D:16%
66	A:100%	B:0%	C:0%	D:0%
67	A:95%	B:5%	C:0%	D:0%
68	A:16%	B:0%	C:0%	D:84%
69	A:0%	B:0%	C:100%	D:0%
70	A:100%	B:0%	C:0%	D:0%
71	A:16%	B:63%	C:16%	D:5%
72	A:84%	B:11%	C:0%	D:5%
73	A:100%	B:0%	C:0%	D:0%
74	A:17%	B:0%	C:83%	D:0%

ASK THE AUDIENCE

75	A:100%	B:0%	C:0%	D:0%	82	A:0%	B:0%	C:100%	D:0%
76	A:96%	B:4%	C:0%	D:0%	83	A:5%	B:90%	C:0%	D:5%
77	A:11%	B:89%	C:0%	D:0%	84	A:100%	B:0%	C:0%	D:0%
78	A:21%	B:10%	C:53%	D:16%	85	A:6%	B:0%	C:94%	D:0%
79	A:0%	B:0%	C:95%	D:5%	86	A:100%	B:0%	C:0%	D:0%
80	A:74%	B:21%	C:0%	D:5%	87	A:0%	B:0%	C:0%	D:100%
81	A:0%	B:6%	C:87%	D:7%	88	A:83%	B:12%	C:5%	D:0%

£200

1	A:6%	B:89%	C:5%	D:0%	33	A:0%	B:87%	C:8%	D:5%
2	A:16%	B:10%	C:0%	D:74%	34	A:0%	B:0%	C:5%	D:95%
3	A:0%	B:0%	C:5%	D:95%	35	A:0%	B:0%	C:95%	D:5%
4	A:5%	B:0%	C:95%	D:0%	36	A:11%	B:0%	C:84%	D:5%
5	A:0%	B:100%	C:0%	D:0%	37	A:5%	B:0%	C:5%	D:90%
6	A:0%	B:5%	C:0%	D:95%	38	A:0%	B:0%	C:0%	D:100%
7	A:11%	B:5%	C:0%	D:84%	39	A:0%	B:0%	C:0%	D:100%
8	A:95%	B:0%	C:5%	D:0%	40	A:5%	B:5%	C:11%	D:79%
9	A:0%	B:0%	C:100%	D:0%	41	A:0%	B:94%	C:0%	D:6%
10	A:0%	B:0%	C:6%	D:94%	42	A:0%	B:95%	C:0%	D:5%
11	A:7%	B:0%	C:93%	D:0%	43	A:74%	B:5%	C:16%	D:5%
12	A:56%	B:28%	C:10%	D:6%	44	A:0%	B:5%	C:95%	D:0%
13	A:6%	B:0%	C:94%	D:0%	45	A:0%	B:7%	C:88%	D:5%
14	A:100%	B:0%	C:0%	D:0%	46	A:95%	B:0%	C:0%	D:5%
15	A:0%	B:0%	C:0%	D:100%	47	A:11%	B:0%	C:89%	D:0%
16	A:22%	B:0%	C:78%	D:0%	48	A:89%	B:0%	C:5%	D:6%
17	A:0%	B:0%	C:89%	D:11%	49	A:0%	B:0%	C:96%	D:4%
18	A:0%	B:5%	C:0%	D:95%	50	A:16%	B:79%	C:0%	D:5%
19	A:6%	B:0%	C:6%	D:88%	51	A:0%	B:87%	C:6%	D:7%
20	A:0%	B:89%	C:5%	D:6%	52	A:68%	B:21%	C:5%	D:6%
21	A:0%	B:0%	C:100%	D:0%	53	A:21%	B:0%	C:11%	D:68%
22	A:100%	B:0%	C:0%	D:0%	54	A:94%	B:6%	C:0%	D:0%
23	A:100%	B:0%	C:0%	D:0%	55	A:6%	B:88%	C:0%	D:6%
24	A:0%	B:0%	C:100%	D:0%	56	A:0%	B:6%	C:94%	D:0%
25	A:0%	B:100%	C:0%	D:0%	57	A:6%	B:5%	C:89%	D:0%
26	A:0%	B:0%	C:16%	D:84%	58	A:0%	B:87%	C:7%	D:6%
27	A:5%	B:0%	C:95%	D:0%	59	A:6%	B:82%	C:6%	D:6%
28	A:0%	B:100%	C:0%	D:0%	60	A:5%	B:6%	C:0%	D:89%
29	A:0%	B:6%	C:94%	D:0%	61	A:0%	B:38%	C:56%	D:6%
30	A:0%	B:7%	C:88%	D:5%	62	A:17%	B:12%	C:0%	D:71%
31	A:0%	B:0%	C:100%	D:0%	63	A:65%	B:18%	C:6%	D:11%
32	A:89%	B:11%	C:0%	D:0%	64	A:82%	B:12%	C:0%	D:6%

ASK THE AUDIENCE

65	A:11%	B:5%	C:79%	D:5%	75	A:0%	B:5%	C:0%	D:95%
66	A:7%	B:0%	C:5%	D:88%	76	A:5%	B:79%	C:0%	D:16%
67	A:5%	B:11%	C:0%	D:84%	77	A:0%	B:0%	C:100%	D:0%
68	A:88%	B:0%	C:6%	D:6%	78	A:0%	B:0%	C:7%	D:93%
69	A:11%	B:89%	C:0%	D:0%	79	A:100%	B:0%	C:0%	D:0%
70	A:0%	B:15%	C:0%	D:83%	80	A:94%	B:0%	C:6%	D:0%
71	A:95%	B:0%	C:5%	D:0%	81	A:0%	B:0%	C:100%	D:0%
72	A:0%	B:100%	C:0%	D:0%	82	A:5%	B:0%	C:0%	D:95%
73	A:0%	B:95%	C:0%	D:5%	83	A:0%	B:95%	C:5%	D:0%
74	A:96%	B:4%	C:0%	D:0%	84	A:0%	B:0%	C:0%	D:100%

£300

1	A:16%	B:5%	C:0%	D:79%	30	A:0%	B:5%	C:7%	D:88%
2	A:0%	B:0%	C:0%	D:100%	31	A:0%	B:0%	C:0%	D:100%
3	A:5%	B:0%	C:0%	D:95%	32	A:21%	B:11%	C:5%	D:63%
4	A:0%	B:0%	C:0%	D:100%	33	A:10%	B:5%	C:74%	D:11%
5	A:11%	B:53%	C:4%	D:32%	34	A:8%	B:0%	C:5%	D:87%
6	A:0%	B:100%	C:0%	D:0%	35	A:11%	B:0%	C:79%	D:10%
7	A:0%	B:0%	C:11%	D:89%	36	A:21%	B:11%	C:5%	D:63%
8	A:0%	B:95%	C:5%	D:0%	37	A:89%	B:11%	C:0%	D:0%
9	A:0%	B:100%	C:0%	D:0%	38	A:100%	B:0%	C:0%	D:0%
10	A:5%	B:0%	C:0%	D:95%	39	A:0%	B:94%	C:0%	D:6%
11	A:5%	B:79%	C:0%	D:16%	40	A:21%	B:0%	C:11%	D:68%
12	A:7%	B:93%	C:0%	D:0%	41	A:0%	B:6%	C:5%	D:89%
13	A:0%	B:95%	C:0%	D:5%	42	A:100%	B:0%	C:0%	D:0%
14	A:16%	B:0%	C:5%	D:79%	43	A:16%	B:79%	C:0%	D:5%
15	A:5%	B:6%	C:89%	D:0%	44	A:21%	B:58%	C:10%	D:11%
16	A:10%	B:5%	C:74%	D:11%	45	A:0%	B:87%	C:6%	D:7%
17	A:74%	B:10%	C:16%	D:0%	46	A:11%	B:0%	C:89%	D:0%
18	A:0%	B:94%	C:0%	D:6%	47	A:0%	B:87%	C:6%	D:7%
19	A:0%	B:7%	C:88%	D:5%	48	A:89%	B:0%	C:5%	D:6%
20	A:0%	B:0%	C:0%	D:100%	49	A:100%	B:0%	C:0%	D:0%
21	A:10%	B:13%	C:65%	D:12%	50	A:6%	B:5%	C:89%	D:0%
22	A:0%	B:8%	C:5%	D:87%	51	A:94%	B:6%	C:0%	D:0%
23	A:0%	B:11%	C:0%	D:89%	52	A:0%	B:5%	C:89%	D:6%
24	A:5%	B:84%	C:0%	D:11%	53	A:10%	B:5%	C:74%	D:11%
25	A:0%	B:95%	C:5%	D:0%	54	A:11%	B:5%	C:79%	D:5%
26	A:89%	B:0%	C:5%	D:6%	55	A:0%	B:6%	C:94%	D:0%
27	A:68%	B:21%	C:5%	D:6%	56	A:0%	B:0%	C:0%	D:100%
28	A:16%	B:79%	C:0%	D:5%	57	A:95%	B:0%	C:5%	D:0%
29	A:6%	B:0%	C:89%	D:5%	58	A:0%	B:87%	C:7%	D:6%

ASK THE AUDIENCE

59	A:5%	B:6%	C:0%	D:89%	70	A:6%	B:0%	C:68%	D:26%
60	A:0%	B:0%	C:0%	D:100%	71	A:0%	B:0%	C:7%	D:93%
61	A:0%	B:38%	C:56%	D:6%	72	A:5%	B:79%	C:0%	D:16%
62	A:65%	B:18%	C:6%	D:11%	73	A:0%	B:95%	C:0%	D:5%
63	A:0%	B:100%	C:0%	D:0%	74	A:0%	B:0%	C:100%	D:0%
64	A:82%	B:12%	C:0%	D:6%	75	A:74%	B:10%	C:16%	D:0%
65	A:11%	B:5%	C:79%	D:5%	76	A:72%	B:5%	C:13%	D:10%
66	A:7%	B:0%	C:5%	D:88%	77	A:89%	B:6%	C:0%	D:5%
67	A:88%	B:0%	C:6%	D:6%	78	A:0%	B:6%	C:68%	D:26%
68	A:6%	B:0%	C:89%	D:5%	79	A:0%	B:68%	C:26%	D:6%
69	A:72%	B:17%	C:6%	D:5%	80	A:100%	B:0%	C:0%	D:0%

£500

1	A:0%	B:89%	C:5%	D:6%	28	A:0%	B:5%	C:0%	D:95%
2	A:26%	B:42%	C:27%	D:5%	29	A:6%	B:0%	C:89%	D:5%
3	A:5%	B:22%	C:67%	D:6%	30	A:0%	B:5%	C:7%	D:88%
4	A:95%	B:0%	C:5%	D:0%	31	A:5%	B:79%	C:0%	D:16%
5	A:0%	B:0%	C:0%	D:100%	32	A:95%	B:0%	C:5%	D:0%
6	A:100%	B:0%	C:0%	D:0%	33	A:0%	B:68%	C:26%	D:6%
7	A:89%	B:11%	C:0%	D:0%	34	A:0%	B:8%	C:5%	D:87%
8	A:95%	B:0%	C:0%	D:5%	35	A:11%	B:0%	C:79%	D:10%
9	A:5%	B:0%	C:53%	D:42%	36	A:42%	B:42%	C:5%	D:11%
10	A:16%	B:5%	C:0%	D:79%	37	A:56%	B:6%	C:17%	D:21%
11	A:79%	B:10%	C:11%	D:0%	38	A:17%	B:0%	C:83%	D:0%
12	A:0%	B:4%	C:96%	D:0%	39	A:21%	B:11%	C:5%	D:63%
13	A:0%	B:6%	C:68%	D:26%	40	A:11%	B:53%	C:4%	D:32%
14	A:95%	B:0%	C:5%	D:0%	41	A:5%	B:11%	C:16%	D:68%
15	A:16%	B:0%	C:5%	D:79%	42	A:10%	B:0%	C:90%	D:0%
16	A:5%	B:6%	C:89%	D:0%	43	A:5%	B:95%	C:0%	D:0%
17	A:4%	B:0%	C:96%	D:0%	44	A:11%	B:0%	C:84%	D:5%
18	A:5%	B:0%	C:0%	D:95%	45	A:0%	B:100%	C:0%	D:0%
19	A:7%	B:93%	C:0%	D:0%	46	A:89%	B:6%	C:0%	D:5%
20	A:37%	B:6%	C:36%	D:21%	47	A:94%	B:0%	C:0%	D:6%
21	A:74%	B:10%	C:16%	D:0%	48	A:11%	B:10%	C:0%	D:79%
22	A:16%	B:0%	C:79%	D:5%	49	A:72%	B:17%	C:6%	D:5%
23	A:90%	B:0%	C:10%	D:0%	50	A:74%	B:5%	C:5%	D:16%
24	A:89%	B:0%	C:0%	D:11%	51	A:79%	B:0%	C:0%	D:21%
25	A:16%	B:37%	C:37%	D:10%	52	A:11%	B:5%	C:21%	D:63%
26	A:0%	B:11%	C:0%	D:89%	53	A:0%	B:95%	C:0%	D:5%
27	A:5%	B:84%	C:0%	D:11%	54	A:0%	B:0%	C:21%	D:79%

ASK THE AUDIENCE

55	A:0%	B:0%	C:6%	D:94%		66	A:0%	B:6%	C:5%	D:89%
56	A:0%	B:37%	C:0%	D:63%		67	A:95%	B:0%	C:5%	D:0%
57	A:0%	B:100%	C:0%	D:0%		68	A:5%	B:89%	C:0%	D:6%
58	A:79%	B:11%	C:5%	D:5%		69	A:10%	B:0%	C:79%	D:11%
59	A:0%	B:5%	C:89%	D:6%		70	A:11%	B:5%	C:0%	D:84%
60	A:16%	B:58%	C:16%	D:10%		71	A:10%	B:5%	C:74%	D:11%
61	A:0%	B:0%	C:5%	D:95%		72	A:63%	B:16%	C:21%	D:0%
62	A:11%	B:0%	C:0%	D:89%		73	A:32%	B:58%	C:10%	D:0%
63	A:0%	B:0%	C:68%	D:32%		74	A:95%	B:0%	C:5%	D:0%
64	A:0%	B:6%	C:89%	D:5%		75	A:0%	B:5%	C:95%	D:0%
65	A:69%	B:5%	C:26%	D:0%		76	A:21%	B:58%	C:10%	D:11%

£1,000

1	A:95%	B:0%	C:5%	D:0%		29	A:21%	B:26%	C:53%	D:0%
2	A:16%	B:68%	C:5%	D:11%		30	A:10%	B:13%	C:65%	D:12%
3	A:68%	B:21%	C:0%	D:11%		31	A:0%	B:84%	C:11%	D:5%
4	A:11%	B:63%	C:16%	D:10%		32	A:5%	B:6%	C:5%	D:84%
5	A:63%	B:0%	C:16%	D:21%		33	A:0%	B:53%	C:42%	D:5%
6	A:26%	B:53%	C:5%	D:16%		34	A:6%	B:72%	C:5%	D:17%
7	A:5%	B:16%	C:53%	D:26%		35	A:0%	B:82%	C:6%	D:12%
8	A:21%	B:11%	C:63%	D:5%		36	A:5%	B:16%	C:5%	D:74%
9	A:21%	B:5%	C:63%	D:11%		37	A:0%	B:5%	C:84%	D:11%
10	A:100%	B:0%	C:0%	D:0%		38	A:0%	B:74%	C:16%	D:10%
11	A:0%	B:0%	C:0%	D:100%		39	A:0%	B:0%	C:88%	D:12%
12	A:0%	B:0%	C:95%	D:5%		40	A:0%	B:11%	C:10%	D:79%
13	A:47%	B:5%	C:11%	D:37%		41	A:0%	B:0%	C:33%	D:67%
14	A:68%	B:6%	C:5%	D:21%		42	A:26%	B:21%	C:21%	D:32%
15	A:37%	B:16%	C:0%	D:47%		43	A:17%	B:67%	C:6%	D:10%
16	A:0%	B:11%	C:26%	D:63%		44	A:0%	B:21%	C:16%	D:63%
17	A:17%	B:6%	C:10%	D:67%		45	A:0%	B:11%	C:5%	D:84%
18	A:17%	B:22%	C:11%	D:50%		46	A:0%	B:79%	C:11%	D:10%
19	A:66%	B:0%	C:6%	D:28%		47	A:5%	B:63%	C:21%	D:11%
20	A:5%	B:17%	C:61%	D:17%		48	A:11%	B:63%	C:10%	D:16%
21	A:12%	B:22%	C:22%	D:44%		49	A:37%	B:5%	C:11%	D:47%
22	A:10%	B:37%	C:53%	D:0%		50	A:6%	B:5%	C:84%	D:5%
23	A:79%	B:11%	C:10%	D:0%		51	A:10%	B:37%	C:42%	D:11%
24	A:11%	B:72%	C:0%	D:17%		52	A:9%	B:38%	C:53%	D:0%
25	A:84%	B:0%	C:0%	D:16%		53	A:100%	B:0%	C:0%	D:0%
26	A:0%	B:11%	C:89%	D:0%		54	A:5%	B:0%	C:56%	D:39%
27	A:10%	B:53%	C:21%	D:16%		55	A:11%	B:0%	C:0%	D:89%
28	A:6%	B:0%	C:89%	D:5%		56	A:27%	B:0%	C:0%	D:73%

ASK THE AUDIENCE

57	A:21%	B:0%	C:5%	D:74%	65	A:6%	B:89%	C:5%	D:0%
58	A:5%	B:11%	C:79%	D:5%	66	A:0%	B:16%	C:10%	D:74%
59	A:5%	B:16%	C:63%	D:16%	67	A:63%	B:21%	C:16%	D:0%
60	A:5%	B:15%	C:75%	D:5%	68	A:21%	B:10%	C:16%	D:53%
61	A:16%	B:10%	C:74%	D:0%	69	A:5%	B:84%	C:5%	D:6%
62	A:16%	B:68%	C:5%	D:11%	70	A:11%	B:6%	C:11%	D:72%
63	A:68%	B:0%	C:32%	D:0%	71	A:16%	B:58%	C:10%	D:16%
64	A:11%	B:10%	C:68%	D:11%	72	A:0%	B:11%	C:0%	D:89%

£2,000

1	A:5%	B:95%	C:0%	D:0%	32	A:5%	B:95%	C:0%	D:0%
2	A:16%	B:68%	C:11%	D:5%	33	A:100%	B:0%	C:0%	D:0%
3	A:17%	B:17%	C:33%	D:33%	34	A:5%	B:5%	C:11%	D:79%
4	A:53%	B:26%	C:16%	D:5%	35	A:32%	B:0%	C:63%	D:5%
5	A:11%	B:26%	C:16%	D:47%	36	A:0%	B:0%	C:90%	D:10%
6	A:5%	B:16%	C:79%	D:0%	37	A:11%	B:0%	C:89%	D:0%
7	A:53%	B:32%	C:11%	D:4%	38	A:84%	B:16%	C:0%	D:0%
8	A:21%	B:26%	C:47%	D:6%	39	A:21%	B:63%	C:5%	D:11%
9	A:47%	B:32%	C:5%	D:16%	40	A:5%	B:95%	C:0%	D:0%
10	A:16%	B:5%	C:21%	D:58%	41	A:37%	B:26%	C:5%	D:32%
11	A:42%	B:26%	C:16%	D:16%	42	A:5%	B:37%	C:47%	D:11%
12	A:11%	B:0%	C:89%	D:0%	43	A:6%	B:6%	C:10%	D:78%
13	A:100%	B:0%	C:0%	D:0%	44	A:18%	B:35%	C:29%	D:18%
14	A:5%	B:79%	C:11%	D:5%	45	A:74%	B:16%	C:10%	D:0%
15	A:47%	B:6%	C:26%	D:21%	46	A:100%	B:0%	C:0%	D:0%
16	A:0%	B:100%	C:0%	D:0%	47	A:11%	B:0%	C:63%	D:26%
17	A:89%	B:6%	C:0%	D:5%	48	A:26%	B:10%	C:53%	D:11%
18	A:84%	B:5%	C:0%	D:11%	49	A:5%	B:68%	C:6%	D:21%
19	A:16%	B:0%	C:79%	D:5%	50	A:32%	B:53%	C:5%	D:10%
20	A:0%	B:0%	C:0%	D:100%	51	A:0%	B:0%	C:16%	D:84%
21	A:7%	B:0%	C:5%	D:88%	52	A:11%	B:47%	C:42%	D:0%
22	A:5%	B:89%	C:0%	D:6%	53	A:6%	B:5%	C:0%	D:89%
23	A:26%	B:53%	C:16%	D:5%	54	A:17%	B:6%	C:61%	D:16%
24	A:32%	B:47%	C:11%	D:10%	55	A:0%	B:100%	C:0%	D:0%
25	A:0%	B:0%	C:21%	D:79%	56	A:28%	B:66%	C:6%	D:0%
26	A:5%	B:0%	C:84%	D:11%	57	A:0%	B:100%	C:0%	D:0%
27	A:95%	B:5%	C:0%	D:0%	58	A:42%	B:16%	C:37%	D:5%
28	A:84%	B:16%	C:0%	D:0%	59	A:5%	B:58%	C:0%	D:37%
29	A:0%	B:84%	C:16%	D:0%	60	A:0%	B:100%	C:0%	D:0%
30	A:11%	B:5%	C:37%	D:47%	61	A:0%	B:0%	C:100%	D:0%
31	A:0%	B:21%	C:63%	D:16%	62	A:6%	B:68%	C:5%	D:21%

ASK THE AUDIENCE

63	A:0%	B:0%	C:0%	D:100%	66	A:0%	B:89%	C:11%	D:0%
64	A:58%	B:21%	C:16%	D:5%	67	A:10%	B:5%	C:53%	D:32%
65	A:11%	B:5%	C:79%	D:5%	68	A:21%	B:0%	C:11%	D:68%

£4,000

1	A:0%	B:11%	C:84%	D:5%	33	A:10%	B:16%	C:37%	D:37%
2	A:63%	B:26%	C:5%	D:6%	34	A:17%	B:67%	C:6%	D:10%
3	A:21%	B:5%	C:53%	D:21%	35	A:16%	B:31%	C:21%	D:32%
4	A:53%	B:10%	C:16%	D:21%	36	A:22%	B:50%	C:6%	D:22%
5	A:79%	B:16%	C:5%	D:0%	37	A:6%	B:61%	C:22%	D:11%
6	A:74%	B:10%	C:16%	D:0%	38	A:47%	B:11%	C:10%	D:32%
7	A:16%	B:42%	C:16%	D:26%	39	A:16%	B:0%	C:63%	D:21%
8	A:17%	B:66%	C:0%	D:17%	40	A:32%	B:37%	C:21%	D:10%
9	A:16%	B:42%	C:26%	D:16%	41	A:10%	B:32%	C:0%	D:58%
10	A:16%	B:16%	C:58%	D:10%	42	A:10%	B:53%	C:21%	D:16%
11	A:47%	B:16%	C:21%	D:16%	43	A:21%	B:0%	C:26%	D:53%
12	A:47%	B:26%	C:11%	D:16%	44	A:42%	B:32%	C:5%	D:21%
13	A:53%	B:16%	C:15%	D:16%	45	A:10%	B:0%	C:74%	D:16%
14	A:22%	B:39%	C:17%	D:22%	46	A:5%	B:63%	C:26%	D:6%
15	A:35%	B:12%	C:41%	D:12%	47	A:11%	B:53%	C:21%	D:15%
16	A:37%	B:26%	C:5%	D:32%	48	A:95%	B:0%	C:0%	D:5%
17	A:0%	B:11%	C:63%	D:26%	49	A:68%	B:5%	C:11%	D:16%
18	A:5%	B:26%	C:32%	D:37%	50	A:21%	B:47%	C:11%	D:21%
19	A:21%	B:16%	C:31%	D:32%	51	A:21%	B:26%	C:16%	D:37%
20	A:5%	B:11%	C:79%	D:5%	52	A:47%	B:5%	C:16%	D:32%
21	A:16%	B:26%	C:26%	D:32%	53	A:21%	B:0%	C:74%	D:5%
22	A:0%	B:11%	C:84%	D:5%	54	A:21%	B:11%	C:26%	D:42%
23	A:42%	B:5%	C:11%	D:42%	55	A:5%	B:0%	C:17%	D:78%
24	A:37%	B:10%	C:16%	D:37%	56	A:11%	B:5%	C:16%	D:68%
25	A:21%	B:11%	C:58%	D:10%	57	A:28%	B:33%	C:28%	D:11%
26	A:32%	B:32%	C:10%	D:26%	58	A:26%	B:53%	C:11%	D:10%
27	A:53%	B:5%	C:0%	D:42%	59	A:0%	B:89%	C:5%	D:6%
28	A:0%	B:79%	C:10%	D:11%	60	A:89%	B:5%	C:0%	D:6%
29	A:5%	B:6%	C:89%	D:0%	61	A:5%	B:10%	C:80%	D:5%
30	A:26%	B:11%	C:5%	D:58%	62	A:6%	B:21%	C:5%	D:68%
31	A:37%	B:15%	C:32%	D:16%	63	A:11%	B:0%	C:84%	D:5%
32	A:5%	B:16%	C:79%	D:0%	64	A:32%	B:5%	C:16%	D:47%

ASK THE AUDIENCE

£8,000

1	A:16%	B:68%	C:5%	D:11%	31	A:72%	B:5%	C:13%	D:10%
2	A:5%	B:21%	C:0%	D:74%	32	A:89%	B:11%	C:0%	D:0%
3	A:26%	B:53%	C:10%	D:11%	33	A:21%	B:0%	C:79%	D:0%
4	A:11%	B:63%	C:0%	D:26%	34	A:21%	B:16%	C:10%	D:53%
5	A:79%	B:10%	C:6%	D:5%	35	A:5%	B:53%	C:10%	D:32%
6	A:0%	B:95%	C:5%	D:0%	36	A:42%	B:26%	C:11%	D:21%
7	A:21%	B:21%	C:11%	D:47%	37	A:21%	B:0%	C:16%	D:63%
8	A:12%	B:5%	C:4%	D:79%	38	A:21%	B:37%	C:16%	D:26%
9	A:53%	B:16%	C:26%	D:5%	39	A:22%	B:17%	C:55%	D:6%
10	A:21%	B:10%	C:26%	D:43%	40	A:16%	B:21%	C:58%	D:5%
11	A:11%	B:42%	C:32%	D:15%	41	A:11%	B:21%	C:10%	D:58%
12	A:68%	B:5%	C:11%	D:16%	42	A:6%	B:28%	C:56%	D:10%
13	A:32%	B:5%	C:63%	D:0%	43	A:26%	B:21%	C:27%	D:26%
14	A:24%	B:18%	C:46%	D:12%	44	A:16%	B:42%	C:5%	D:37%
15	A:0%	B:32%	C:58%	D:10%	45	A:5%	B:5%	C:79%	D:11%
16	A:16%	B:68%	C:16%	D:0%	46	A:100%	B:0%	C:0%	D:0%
17	A:0%	B:21%	C:0%	D:79%	47	A:16%	B:5%	C:16%	D:63%
18	A:10%	B:0%	C:16%	D:74%	48	A:6%	B:47%	C:42%	D:5%
19	A:63%	B:0%	C:16%	D:21%	49	A:26%	B:58%	C:5%	D:11%
20	A:53%	B:11%	C:10%	D:26%	50	A:5%	B:0%	C:95%	D:0%
21	A:0%	B:0%	C:100%	D:0%	51	A:79%	B:16%	C:5%	D:0%
22	A:11%	B:50%	C:11%	D:28%	52	A:0%	B:95%	C:5%	D:0%
23	A:0%	B:6%	C:18%	D:76%	53	A:13%	B:10%	C:44%	D:33%
24	A:58%	B:26%	C:5%	D:11%	54	A:28%	B:22%	C:0%	D:50%
25	A:6%	B:56%	C:10%	D:28%	55	A:47%	B:26%	C:5%	D:22%
26	A:21%	B:53%	C:5%	D:21%	56	A:26%	B:0%	C:16%	D:58%
27	A:5%	B:0%	C:11%	D:84%	57	A:5%	B:21%	C:63%	D:11%
28	A:63%	B:0%	C:10%	D:27%	58	A:26%	B:74%	C:0%	D:0%
29	A:0%	B:89%	C:6%	D:5%	59	A:42%	B:26%	C:27%	D:5%
30	A:6%	B:83%	C:0%	D:11%	60	A:43%	B:16%	C:15%	D:26%

£16,000

1	A:100%	B:0%	C:0%	D:0%	9	A:0%	B:0%	C:79%	D:21%
2	A:5%	B:6%	C:84%	D:5%	10	A:0%	B:83%	C:11%	D:6%
3	A:74%	B:0%	C:5%	D:21%	11	A:0%	B:100%	C:0%	D:0%
4	A:6%	B:11%	C:57%	D:26%	12	A:0%	B:5%	C:95%	D:0%
5	A:4%	B:96%	C:0%	D:0%	13	A:4%	B:96%	C:0%	D:0%
6	A:0%	B:0%	C:0%	D:100%	14	A:47%	B:5%	C:48%	D:0%
7	A:11%	B:32%	C:53%	D:4%	15	A:0%	B:6%	C:5%	D:89%
8	A:10%	B:4%	C:5%	D:81%	16	A:21%	B:22%	C:47%	D:10%

ASK THE AUDIENCE

17	A:0%	B:0%	C:89%	D:11%
18	A:5%	B:0%	C:95%	D:0%
19	A:0%	B:6%	C:89%	D:5%
20	A:21%	B:42%	C:11%	D:26%
21	A:0%	B:0%	C:100%	D:0%
22	A:11%	B:68%	C:16%	D:5%
23	A:32%	B:21%	C:10%	D:37%
24	A:10%	B:16%	C:11%	D:63%
25	A:21%	B:42%	C:37%	D:0%
26	A:100%	B:0%	C:0%	D:0%
27	A:0%	B:21%	C:79%	D:0%
28	A:21%	B:5%	C:0%	D:74%
29	A:16%	B:79%	C:0%	D:5%
30	A:58%	B:0%	C:16%	D:26%
31	A:53%	B:20%	C:16%	D:11%
32	A:42%	B:27%	C:5%	D:26%
33	A:21%	B:11%	C:10%	D:58%
34	A:53%	B:16%	C:15%	D:16%
35	A:75%	B:5%	C:10%	D:10%
36	A:26%	B:0%	C:62%	D:12%

37	A:16%	B:16%	C:32%	D:36%
38	A:32%	B:21%	C:16%	D:31%
39	A:0%	B:20%	C:53%	D:27%
40	A:21%	B:21%	C:26%	D:32%
41	A:32%	B:11%	C:37%	D:20%
42	A:68%	B:21%	C:0%	D:11%
43	A:68%	B:5%	C:10%	D:17%
44	A:95%	B:0%	C:0%	D:5%
45	A:5%	B:0%	C:79%	D:16%
46	A:0%	B:5%	C:78%	D:17%
47	A:21%	B:16%	C:63%	D:0%
48	A:58%	B:31%	C:0%	D:11%
49	A:58%	B:32%	C:5%	D:5%
50	A:31%	B:37%	C:6%	D:26%
51	A:5%	B:95%	C:0%	D:0%
52	A:26%	B:32%	C:16%	D:26%
53	A:84%	B:11%	C:5%	D:0%
54	A:26%	B:27%	C:26%	D:21%
55	A:68%	B:11%	C:10%	D:11%
56	A:32%	B:0%	C:63%	D:5%

£32,000

1	A:37%	B:21%	C:16%	D:26%
2	A:5%	B:59%	C:11%	D:25%
3	A:0%	B:21%	C:74%	D:5%
4	A:0%	B:5%	C:95%	D:0%
5	A:53%	B:21%	C:6%	D:20%
6	A:11%	B:68%	C:5%	D:16%
7	A:21%	B:31%	C:16%	D:32%
8	A:16%	B:47%	C:11%	D:26%
9	A:16%	B:63%	C:10%	D:11%
10	A:6%	B:11%	C:0%	D:83%
11	A:42%	B:10%	C:32%	D:16%
12	A:22%	B:67%	C:5%	D:6%
13	A:68%	B:16%	C:6%	D:10%
14	A:0%	B:74%	C:5%	D:21%
15	A:11%	B:31%	C:26%	D:32%
16	A:22%	B:22%	C:39%	D:17%
17	A:32%	B:5%	C:32%	D:31%
18	A:32%	B:16%	C:5%	D:47%
19	A:26%	B:32%	C:16%	D:26%

20	A:21%	B:5%	C:42%	D:32%
21	A:51%	B:12%	C:5%	D:32%
22	A:11%	B:10%	C:32%	D:47%
23	A:10%	B:34%	C:17%	D:39%
24	A:10%	B:32%	C:42%	D:16%
25	A:47%	B:32%	C:16%	D:5%
26	A:12%	B:32%	C:17%	D:39%
27	A:48%	B:21%	C:16%	D:15%
28	A:74%	B:15%	C:6%	D:5%
29	A:61%	B:0%	C:33%	D:6%
30	A:37%	B:0%	C:47%	D:16%
31	A:16%	B:32%	C:26%	D:26%
32	A:32%	B:57%	C:5%	D:6%
33	A:0%	B:74%	C:21%	D:5%
34	A:10%	B:53%	C:0%	D:37%
35	A:11%	B:0%	C:68%	D:21%
36	A:28%	B:44%	C:17%	D:11%
37	A:21%	B:32%	C:16%	D:31%
38	A:21%	B:6%	C:47%	D:26%

ASK THE AUDIENCE

39	A:5%	B:11%	C:16%	D:68%	46	A:26%	B:21%	C:25%	D:28%
40	A:6%	B:26%	C:5%	D:63%	47	A:37%	B:16%	C:26%	D:21%
41	A:11%	B:15%	C:16%	D:58%	48	A:58%	B:15%	C:16%	D:11%
42	A:10%	B:32%	C:21%	D:37%	49	A:28%	B:39%	C:22%	D:11%
43	A:50%	B:11%	C:17%	D:22%	50	A:10%	B:28%	C:6%	D:56%
44	A:10%	B:58%	C:6%	D:26%	51	A:0%	B:47%	C:42%	D:11%
45	A:32%	B:16%	C:37%	D:15%	52	A:32%	B:37%	C:16%	D:15%

£64,000

1	A:21%	B:11%	C:26%	D:42%	25	A:5%	B:21%	C:16%	D:58%
2	A:63%	B:0%	C:12%	D:25%	26	A:53%	B:20%	C:5%	D:22%
3	A:16%	B:16%	C:10%	D:58%	27	A:32%	B:47%	C:11%	D:10%
4	A:32%	B:5%	C:37%	D:26%	28	A:0%	B:69%	C:21%	D:10%
5	A:10%	B:37%	C:37%	D:16%	29	A:5%	B:6%	C:0%	D:89%
6	A:0%	B:10%	C:79%	D:11%	30	A:48%	B:21%	C:11%	D:20%
7	A:0%	B:100%	C:0%	D:0%	31	A:5%	B:47%	C:32%	D:16%
8	A:47%	B:26%	C:22%	D:5%	32	A:38%	B:26%	C:10%	D:26%
9	A:21%	B:53%	C:10%	D:16%	33	A:42%	B:0%	C:32%	D:26%
10	A:5%	B:16%	C:58%	D:21%	34	A:21%	B:26%	C:42%	D:11%
11	A:0%	B:5%	C:11%	D:84%	35	A:26%	B:47%	C:21%	D:6%
12	A:21%	B:16%	C:26%	D:37%	36	A:26%	B:21%	C:32%	D:21%
13	A:16%	B:21%	C:47%	D:16%	37	A:32%	B:16%	C:15%	D:37%
14	A:16%	B:67%	C:12%	D:5%	38	A:5%	B:58%	C:5%	D:32%
15	A:5%	B:21%	C:26%	D:48%	39	A:33%	B:22%	C:17%	D:28%
16	A:74%	B:5%	C:16%	D:5%	40	A:25%	B:31%	C:19%	D:25%
17	A:42%	B:36%	C:10%	D:12%	41	A:89%	B:5%	C:0%	D:6%
18	A:21%	B:23%	C:21%	D:35%	42	A:84%	B:5%	C:6%	D:5%
19	A:11%	B:20%	C:53%	D:16%	43	A:33%	B:44%	C:12%	D:11%
20	A:32%	B:26%	C:12%	D:30%	44	A:11%	B:0%	C:0%	D:89%
21	A:10%	B:42%	C:32%	D:16%	45	A:5%	B:12%	C:57%	D:26%
22	A:5%	B:79%	C:10%	D:6%	46	A:21%	B:21%	C:11%	D:47%
23	A:7%	B:16%	C:72%	D:5%	47	A:37%	B:5%	C:21%	D:37%
24	A:21%	B:0%	C:42%	D:37%	48	A:26%	B:16%	C:16%	D:42%

£125,000

1	A:63%	B:16%	C:5%	D:16%	5	A:5%	B:11%	C:21%	D:63%
2	A:79%	B:5%	C:5%	D:11%	6	A:5%	B:0%	C:84%	D:11%
3	A:9%	B:74%	C:12%	D:5%	7	A:22%	B:22%	C:12%	D:44%
4	A:11%	B:42%	C:21%	D:26%	8	A:12%	B:9%	C:42%	D:37%

ASK THE AUDIENCE

9	A:5%	B:26%	C:48%	D:21%	27	A:32%	B:5%	C:37%	D:26%
10	A:11%	B:61%	C:22%	D:6%	28	A:17%	B:50%	C:11%	D:22%
11	A:50%	B:11%	C:17%	D:22%	29	A:0%	B:63%	C:37%	D:0%
12	A:6%	B:89%	C:0%	D:5%	30	A:21%	B:26%	C:32%	D:21%
13	A:17%	B:78%	C:5%	D:0%	31	A:53%	B:21%	C:20%	D:6%
14	A:28%	B:27%	C:17%	D:28%	32	A:42%	B:32%	C:10%	D:16%
15	A:33%	B:28%	C:23%	D:16%	33	A:41%	B:22%	C:32%	D:5%
16	A:28%	B:22%	C:28%	D:22%	34	A:0%	B:21%	C:26%	D:53%
17	A:37%	B:5%	C:32%	D:26%	35	A:42%	B:37%	C:21%	D:0%
18	A:32%	B:42%	C:10%	D:16%	36	A:53%	B:26%	C:10%	D:11%
19	A:28%	B:39%	C:11%	D:22%	37	A:21%	B:47%	C:16%	D:16%
20	A:42%	B:16%	C:10%	D:32%	38	A:26%	B:26%	C:37%	D:11%
21	A:5%	B:47%	C:11%	D:37%	39	A:5%	B:11%	C:16%	D:68%
22	A:47%	B:22%	C:21%	D:10%	40	A:21%	B:26%	C:26%	D:27%
23	A:16%	B:21%	C:32%	D:31%	41	A:37%	B:21%	C:26%	D:16%
24	A:12%	B:21%	C:21%	D:46%	42	A:21%	B:18%	C:35%	D:26%
25	A:11%	B:47%	C:21%	D:21%	43	A:32%	B:15%	C:37%	D:16%
26	A:53%	B:26%	C:10%	D:11%	44	A:68%	B:16%	C:16%	B:0%

£250,000

1	A:16%	B:15%	C:16%	D:53%	21	A:31%	B:23%	C:18%	D:28%
2	A:26%	B:11%	C:31%	D:32%	22	A:50%	B:22%	C:17%	D:11%
3	A:31%	B:5%	C:53%	D:11%	23	A:37%	B:21%	C:11%	D:31%
4	A:21%	B:21%	C:37%	D:21%	24	A:41%	B:5%	C:33%	D:21%
5	A:37%	B:31%	C:21%	D:11%	25	A:21%	B:16%	C:37%	D:26%
6	A:21%	B:20%	C:37%	D:22%	26	A:21%	B:21%	C:47%	D:11%
7	A:37%	B:21%	C:37%	D:5%	27	A:33%	B:22%	C:33%	D:12%
8	A:32%	B:30%	C:32%	D:6%	28	A:16%	B:21%	C:42%	D:21%
9	A:30%	B:32%	C:16%	D:22%	29	A:17%	B:11%	C:16%	D:56%
10	A:21%	B:26%	C:32%	D:21%	30	A:61%	B:17%	C:22%	D:0%
11	A:32%	B:21%	C:31%	D:16%	31	A:32%	B:16%	C:32%	D:20%
12	A:21%	B:5%	C:32%	D:42%	32	A:28%	B:27%	C:34%	D:11%
13	A:26%	B:16%	C:37%	D:21%	33	A:26%	B:47%	C:11%	D:16%
14	A:16%	B:32%	C:21%	D:31%	34	A:5%	B:21%	C:32%	D:42%
15	A:5%	B:68%	C:11%	D:16%	35	A:5%	B:21%	C:32%	D:42%
16	A:11%	B:26%	C:26%	D:37%	36	A:21%	B:32%	C:26%	D:21%
17	A:37%	B:21%	C:21%	D:21%	37	A:20%	B:32%	C:21%	D:27%
18	A:32%	B:26%	C:21%	D:21%	38	A:21%	B:37%	C:16%	D:26%
19	A:36%	B:11%	C:21%	D:32%	39	A:39%	B:33%	C:11%	D:17%
20	A:21%	B:21%	C:16%	D:42%	40	A:32%	B:11%	C:10%	D:47%

ASK THE AUDIENCE

£500,000

1	A:11%	B:26%	C:37%	D:26%	19	A:6%	B:11%	C:50%	D:33%
2	A:26%	B:5%	C:37%	D:32%	20	A:28%	B:18%	C:42%	D:12%
3	A:32%	B:42%	C:21%	D:5%	21	A:17%	B:11%	C:44%	D:28%
4	A:16%	B:16%	C:47%	D:21%	22	A:18%	B:22%	C:21%	D:39%
5	A:53%	B:16%	C:10%	D:21%	23	A:17%	B:16%	C:18%	D:49%
6	A:10%	B:42%	C:43%	D:5%	24	A:16%	B:39%	C:17%	D:28%
7	A:11%	B:26%	C:47%	D:16%	25	A:32%	B:5%	C:53%	D:10%
8	A:26%	B:11%	C:5%	D:58%	26	A:22%	B:12%	C:33%	D:33%
9	A:42%	B:5%	C:32%	D:21%	27	A:21%	B:16%	C:37%	D:26%
10	A:16%	B:16%	C:21%	D:47%	28	A:21%	B:21%	C:21%	D:37%
11	A:10%	B:32%	C:26%	D:32%	29	A:26%	B:32%	C:21%	D:21%
12	A:16%	B:37%	C:21%	D:26%	30	A:26%	B:10%	C:32%	D:32%
13	A:26%	B:16%	C:21%	D:37%	31	A:26%	B:16%	C:37%	D:21%
14	A:42%	B:32%	C:16%	D:10%	32	A:32%	B:26%	C:26%	D:16%
15	A:11%	B:42%	C:26%	D:21%	33	A:16%	B:21%	C:0%	D:63%
16	A:5%	B:37%	C:32%	D:26%	34	A:37%	B:21%	C:10%	D:32%
17	A:16%	B:42%	C:21%	D:21%	35	A:11%	B:26%	C:16%	D:47%
18	A:55%	B:17%	C:18%	D:10%	36	A:10%	B:37%	C:32%	D:21%

£1,000,000

1	A:16%	B:26%	C:47%	D:11%	17	A:21%	B:26%	C:26%	D:27%
2	A:32%	B:5%	C:53%	D:10%	18	A:21%	B:58%	C:16%	D:5%
3	A:74%	B:5%	C:10%	D:11%	19	A:32%	B:5%	C:47%	D:16%
4	A:16%	B:74%	C:10%	D:0%	20	A:42%	B:6%	C:37%	D:15%
5	A:63%	B:5%	C:6%	D:26%	21	A:22%	B:33%	C:28%	D:17%
6	A:11%	B:21%	C:26%	D:42%	22	A:21%	B:16%	C:42%	D:21%
7	A:10%	B:21%	C:53%	D:16%	23	A:5%	B:11%	C:26%	D:58%
8	A:32%	B:16%	C:20%	D:32%	24	A:6%	B:21%	C:47%	D:26%
9	A:26%	B:26%	C:26%	D:22%	25	A:17%	B:39%	C:10%	D:34%
10	A:16%	B:32%	C:20%	D:32%	26	A:26%	B:21%	C:42%	D:11%
11	A:22%	B:23%	C:44%	D:11%	27	A:11%	B:33%	C:56%	D:0%
12	A:16%	B:37%	C:47%	D:0%	28	A:26%	B:16%	C:37%	D:21%
13	A:21%	B:47%	C:16%	D:16%	29	A:37%	B:15%	C:32%	D:16%
14	A:42%	B:16%	C:21%	D:21%	30	A:11%	B:39%	C:22%	D:28%
15	A:33%	B:28%	C:33%	D:6%	31	A:5%	B:22%	C:26%	D:47%
16	A:21%	B:37%	C:21%	D:21%	32	A:11%	B:32%	C:25%	D:32%

Answers

Fastest Finger First

1	DCAB	2	BCDA	3	ADBC	4	DCAB	5	BCAD
6	CDAB	7	BCDA	8	BCDA	9	BDAC	10	CBDA
11	BADC	12	CDBA	13	DACB	14	CDBA	15	BCDA
16	BADC	17	ACDB	18	CBDA	19	ACDB	20	CDBA
21	DCAB	22	ABDC	23	CABD	24	DCBA	25	DCBA
26	CDAB	27	DACB	28	ADCB	29	BCDA	30	ADCB
31	BCAD	32	DBCA	33	CBAD	34	ADCB	35	ACDB
36	DBCA	37	ADCB	38	CADB	39	ABDC	40	ADCB
41	DABC	42	ACBD	43	CDAB	44	DCAB	45	BACD
46	ADCB	47	BCDA	48	DABC	49	ADBC	50	CDBA
51	DCAB	52	BADC	53	BDCA	54	ADBC	55	ADCB
56	CDBA	57	DCBA	58	DCAB	59	CDAB	60	CBAD
61	DCAB	62	BDAC	63	BDAC	64	DACB	65	CBDA
66	CBAD	67	CDAB	68	CDBA	69	BDCA	70	ADBC
71	BADC	72	DACB	73	CBDA	74	DBCA	75	DACB
76	BACD	77	CBDA	78	ADBC	79	DBAC	80	ACBD
81	ABDC	82	DBAC	83	CADB	84	DBAC	85	BACD
86	CBDA	87	BCDA	88	BDAC	89	CADB	90	BDAC
91	DCAB	92	CDBA	93	CBAD	94	BDAC	95	DBCA
96	BDCA	97	DCAB	98	DCAB	99	ADCB	100	DBAC

If you answered correctly, well done! Turn to page 31 to play for £100!

£100

1	C	2	D	3	D	4	D	5	A	6	B	7	B
8	B	9	C	10	D	11	B	12	B	13	B	14	A
15	C	16	A	17	C	18	A	19	D	20	B	21	C
22	C	23	D	24	C	25	B	26	B	27	B	28	A
29	B	30	B	31	D	32	A	33	A	34	D	35	B
36	D	37	A	38	C	39	D	40	C	41	A	42	D
43	D	44	B	45	C	46	C	47	C	48	D	49	A
50	D	51	D	52	C	53	D	54	D	55	D	56	A

ANSWERS

57 D	58 B	59 C	60 C	61 B	62 A	63 A
64 B	65 A	66 A	67 A	68 D	69 C	70 A
71 B	72 A	73 A	74 C	75 A	76 A	77 B
78 C	79 C	80 A	81 C	82 C	83 B	84 A
85 C	86 A	87 D	88 A			

If you have won £100, well done! Turn to page 51 to play for £200!

£200

1 B	2 D	3 D	4 C	5 B	6 D	7 D
8 A	9 C	10 D	11 C	12 A	13 C	14 A
15 D	16 C	17 C	18 D	19 D	20 B	21 C
22 A	23 A	24 C	25 B	26 D	27 C	28 B
29 C	30 C	31 C	32 A	33 B	34 D	35 C
36 C	37 D	38 D	39 D	40 D	41 B	42 B
43 A	44 C	45 C	46 A	47 C	48 A	49 C
50 B	51 B	52 A	53 D	54 A	55 B	56 C
57 C	58 B	59 B	60 D	61 C	62 D	63 A
64 A	65 C	66 D	67 D	68 A	69 B	70 D
71 A	72 B	73 B	74 A	75 D	76 B	77 C
78 D	79 A	80 A	81 C	82 D	83 B	84 D

If you have won £200, well done! Turn to page 69 to play for £300!

£300

1 D	2 D	3 D	4 D	5 B	6 C	7 D
8 B	9 B	10 D	11 B	12 B	13 B	14 D
15 C	16 C	17 A	18 B	19 C	20 D	21 C
22 D	23 D	24 B	25 B	26 A	27 A	28 B
29 C	30 D	31 D	32 D	33 C	34 D	35 C
36 D	37 A	38 A	39 B	40 D	41 D	42 A
43 B	44 B	45 B	46 C	47 B	48 A	49 A
50 C	51 A	52 C	53 C	54 C	55 C	56 D
57 A	58 B	59 D	60 D	61 C	62 A	63 B
64 A	65 C	66 D	67 A	68 C	69 A	70 C
71 D	72 B	73 B	74 C	75 A	76 A	77 A
78 C	79 B	80 A				

If you have won £300, well done! Turn to page 87 to play for £500!

ANSWERS

£500

1	B	2	B	3	C	4	A	5	D	6	A	7	A
8	A	9	C	10	D	11	A	12	C	13	C	14	A
15	D	16	C	17	C	18	D	19	B	20	C	21	A
22	C	23	A	24	A	25	B	26	D	27	B	28	D
29	C	30	D	31	B	32	A	33	B	34	D	35	C
36	B	37	A	38	C	39	D	40	B	41	D	42	C
43	B	44	C	45	B	46	A	47	A	48	D	49	A
50	A	51	A	52	D	53	B	54	D	55	D	56	B
57	B	58	A	59	C	60	B	61	D	62	D	63	C
64	C	65	A	66	D	67	A	68	B	69	C	70	D
71	C	72	A	73	B	74	A	75	C	76	B		

If you have won £500, well done! Turn to page 105 to play for £1,000!

£1,000

1	A	2	B	3	A	4	B	5	A	6	B	7	C
8	C	9	C	10	A	11	D	12	C	13	A	14	A
15	D	16	D	17	D	18	D	19	A	20	C	21	C
22	C	23	A	24	B	25	A	26	C	27	B	28	C
29	C	30	C	31	B	32	D	33	B	34	B	35	B
36	D	37	C	38	B	39	C	40	D	41	C	42	B
43	B	44	D	45	D	46	B	47	B	48	B	49	A
50	C	51	B	52	C	53	A	54	C	55	D	56	D
57	D	58	C	59	C	60	C	61	C	62	B	63	C
64	C	65	B	66	D	67	A	68	D	69	B	70	D
71	B	72	D										

If you have won £1,000, well done! Turn to page 121 to play for £2,000!

£2,000

1	B	2	B	3	D	4	A	5	D	6	C	7	A
8	C	9	A	10	D	11	A	12	C	13	A	14	B
15	A	16	B	17	A	18	A	19	C	20	D	21	D
22	B	23	C	24	B	25	D	26	C	27	A	28	A
29	B	30	D	31	C	32	B	33	A	34	D	35	C
36	C	37	C	38	A	39	B	40	B	41	B	42	C
43	D	44	B	45	A	46	A	47	D	48	C	49	B
50	B	51	D	52	B	53	D	54	C	55	B	56	B
57	B	58	C	59	D	60	B	61	C	62	B	63	D
64	A	65	C	66	B	67	C	68	D				

If you have won £2,000, well done! Turn to page 137 to play for £4,000!

ANSWERS

£4,000

1	C	2	A	3	C	4	A	5	A	6	A	7	D
8	B	9	D	10	C	11	D	12	B	13	A	14	D
15	A	16	D	17	C	18	D	19	D	20	C	21	C
22	C	23	A	24	A	25	C	26	A	27	D	28	B
29	C	30	D	31	A	32	C	33	D	34	B	35	B
36	B	37	C	38	A	39	C	40	B	41	D	42	B
43	C	44	B	45	C	46	B	47	B	48	A	49	A
50	B	51	D	52	A	53	C	54	A	55	D	56	B
57	B	58	B	59	B	60	A	61	C	62	D	63	C
64	D												

If you have won £4,000, well done! Turn to page 151 to play for £8,000!

£8,000

1	B	2	D	3	B	4	B	5	A	6	B	7	D
8	D	9	B	10	D	11	B	12	D	13	C	14	A
15	C	16	B	17	D	18	D	19	C	20	A	21	C
22	A	23	D	24	A	25	B	26	B	27	D	28	A
29	B	30	B	31	A	32	A	33	C	34	A	35	B
36	A	37	D	38	C	39	C	40	C	41	D	42	C
43	C	44	B	45	C	46	A	47	D	48	C	49	B
50	C	51	A	52	B	53	C	54	D	55	D	56	A
57	C	58	B	59	A	60	A						

If you have won £8,000, well done! Turn to page 165 to play for £16,000!

£16,000

1	A	2	C	3	A	4	C	5	B	6	D	7	C
8	D	9	C	10	B	11	B	12	C	13	B	14	C
15	D	16	C	17	C	18	C	19	C	20	B	21	C
22	B	23	D	24	D	25	B	26	A	27	C	28	D
29	B	30	A	31	A	32	B	33	D	34	A	35	B
36	C	37	C	38	B	39	C	40	B	41	C	42	A
43	A	44	A	45	C	46	C	47	C	48	B	49	A
50	B	51	B	52	B	53	A	54	D	55	A	56	C

If you have won £16,000, well done! Turn to page 179 to play for £32,000!

ANSWERS

£32,000

1	B	2	B	3	C	4	C	5	B	6	B	7	D
8	B	9	B	10	D	11	A	12	B	13	A	14	B
15	D	16	C	17	C	18	D	19	B	20	C	21	A
22	D	23	B	24	C	25	B	26	B	27	B	28	A
29	A	30	B	31	B	32	D	33	B	34	D	35	C
36	C	37	D	38	C	39	D	40	D	41	D	42	A
43	C	44	D	45	A	46	A	47	C	48	C	49	A
50	D	51	C	52	A									

If you have won £32,000, well done! Turn to page 191 to play for £64,000!

£64,000

1	D	2	A	3	D	4	A	5	C	6	C	7	B
8	A	9	B	10	C	11	D	12	D	13	C	14	B
15	B	16	A	17	B	18	C	19	C	20	D	21	B
22	B	23	C	24	C	25	D	26	A	27	B	28	B
29	D	30	A	31	C	32	A	33	A	34	C	35	B
36	A	37	D	38	B	39	A	40	D	41	A	42	A
43	B	44	D	45	C	46	B	47	C	48	D		

If you have won £64,000, well done! Turn to page 203 to play for £125,000!

£125,000

1	A	2	A	3	B	4	B	5	D	6	C	7	D
8	C	9	C	10	B	11	A	12	B	13	B	14	A
15	C	16	A	17	A	18	B	19	B	20	A	21	B
22	A	23	D	24	C	25	B	26	B	27	A	28	B
29	B	30	C	31	A	32	A	33	A	34	D	35	A
36	A	37	B	38	C	39	D	40	B	41	A	42	C
43	C	44	A										

If you have won £125,000, well done! Turn to page 213 to play for £250,000!

£250,000

1	C	2	D	3	A	4	A	5	A	6	C	7	B
8	C	9	B	10	B	11	D	12	A	13	C	14	B
15	B	16	D	17	A	18	A	19	D	20	C	21	A
22	A	23	A	24	A	25	D	26	C	27	C	28	A
29	D	30	A	31	B	32	B	33	D	34	D	35	D
36	C	37	A	38	D	39	D	40	D				

If you have won £250,000, well done! Turn to page 223 to play for £500,000!

ANSWERS

£500,000

1	A	2	B	3	B	4	C	5	A	6	B	7	C
8	D	9	A	10	D	11	C	12	B	13	C	14	A
15	B	16	D	17	B	18	A	19	A	20	A	21	D
22	D	23	B	24	C	25	D	26	A	27	C	28	B
29	D	30	D	31	D	32	D	33	A	34	A	35	C
36	C												

If you have won £500,000, well done! Turn to page 233 to play for £1,000,000!

£1,000,000

1	C	2	C	3	A	4	C	5	A	6	A	7	C
8	A	9	A	10	A	11	A	12	B	13	A	14	A
15	A	16	D	17	C	18	A	19	D	20	C	21	B
22	A	23	D	24	B	25	C	26	A	27	C	28	A
29	D	30	B	31	C	32	A								

If you have won £1,000,000, well done! You're a millionaire!

Score sheets

Write your name and the names of any other contestants in the space provided. Shade in each of the boxes lightly with a pencil once you or one of your fellow contestants has won the amount in that box. If you or any of the other contestants answer a question incorrectly and are out of the game, use a soft eraser to rub out the relevant boxes so that the final score is showing.

SCORE SHEET

contestant's name	contestant's name
....	....
50:50 📞 👥	50:50 📞 👥
☐ ☐ ☐	☐ ☐ ☐

15	£1 MILLION		15	£1 MILLION
14	£500,000		14	£500,000
13	£250,000		13	£250,000
12	£125,000		12	£125,000
11	£64,000		11	£64,000
10	£32,000		10	£32,000
9	£16,000		9	£16,000
8	£8,000		8	£8,000
7	£4,000		7	£4,000
6	£2,000		6	£2,000
5	£1,000		5	£1,000
4	£500		4	£500
3	£300		3	£300
2	£200		2	£200
1	£100		1	£100

SCORE SHEET

contestant's name	contestant's name
....	....

50:50	☎	👥		50:50	☎	👥
☐	☐	☐		☐	☐	☐

15	£1 MILLION		15	£1 MILLION
14	£500,000		14	£500,000
13	£250,000		13	£250,000
12	£125,000		12	£125,000
11	£64,000		11	£64,000
10	£32,000		10	£32,000
9	£16,000		9	£16,000
8	£8,000		8	£8,000
7	£4,000		7	£4,000
6	£2,000		6	£2,000
5	£1,000		5	£1,000
4	£500		4	£500
3	£300		3	£300
2	£200		2	£200
1	£100		1	£100

SCORE SHEET

contestant's name	contestant's name
....	....

50:50	🎙️	👥	50:50	🎙️	👥
☐	☐	☐	☐	☐	☐

15	£1 MILLION	15	£1 MILLION
14	£500,000	14	£500,000
13	£250,000	13	£250,000
12	£125,000	12	£125,000
11	£64,000	11	£64,000
10	£32,000	10	£32,000
9	£16,000	9	£16,000
8	£8,000	8	£8,000
7	£4,000	7	£4,000
6	£2,000	6	£2,000
5	£1,000	5	£1,000
4	£500	4	£500
3	£300	3	£300
2	£200	2	£200
1	£100	1	£100

SCORE SHEET

contestant's name		contestant's name	
....		....	

50:50	☎	👥	50:50	☎	👥
☐	☐	☐	☐	☐	☐

15	£1 MILLION	15	£1 MILLION
14	£500,000	14	£500,000
13	£250,000	13	£250,000
12	£125,000	12	£125,000
11	£64,000	11	£64,000
10	£32,000	**10**	£32,000
9	£16,000	9	£16,000
8	£8,000	8	£8,000
7	£4,000	7	£4,000
6	£2,000	6	£2,000
5	£1,000	**5**	£1,000
4	£500	4	£500
3	£300	3	£300
2	£200	2	£200
1	£100	1	£100

SCORE SHEET

contestant's name	contestant's name
....	....

50:50	☎	👥		50:50	☎	👥
☐	☐	☐		☐	☐	☐

15	£1 MILLION		15	£1 MILLION
14	£500,000		14	£500,000
13	£250,000		13	£250,000
12	£125,000		12	£125,000
11	£64,000		11	£64,000
10	£32,000		10	£32,000
9	£16,000		9	£16,000
8	£8,000		8	£8,000
7	£4,000		7	£4,000
6	£2,000		6	£2,000
5	£1,000		5	£1,000
4	£500		4	£500
3	£300		3	£300
2	£200		2	£200
1	£100		1	£100

SCORE SHEET

15	£1 MILLION	15	£1 MILLION
14	£500,000	14	£500,000
13	£250,000	13	£250,000
12	£125,000	12	£125,000
11	£64,000	11	£64,000
10	£32,000	10	£32,000
9	£16,000	9	£16,000
8	£8,000	8	£8,000
7	£4,000	7	£4,000
6	£2,000	6	£2,000
5	£1,000	5	£1,000
4	£500	4	£500
3	£300	3	£300
2	£200	2	£200
1	£100	1	£100

SCORE SHEET

50:50 · 📞 · 👥👥👥 □ □ □   50:50 · 📞 · 👥👥👥 □ □ □

15	£1 MILLION	15	£1 MILLION
14	£500,000	14	£500,000
13	£250,000	13	£250,000
12	£125,000	12	£125,000
11	£64,000	11	£64,000
10	£32,000	10	£32,000
9	£16,000	9	£16,000
8	£8,000	8	£8,000
7	£4,000	7	£4,000
6	£2,000	6	£2,000
5	£1,000	5	£1,000
4	£500	4	£500
3	£300	3	£300
2	£200	2	£200
1	£100	1	£100

S C O R E   S H E E T

contestant's name	contestant's name
....	....

50:50	☎	👥		50:50	☎	👥
☐	☐	☐		☐	☐	☐

15	£1 MILLION	15	£1 MILLION
14	£500,000	14	£500,000
13	£250,000	13	£250,000
12	£125,000	12	£125,000
11	£64,000	11	£64,000
10	£32,000	**10**	£32,000
9	£16,000	9	£16,000
8	£8,000	8	£8,000
7	£4,000	7	£4,000
6	£2,000	6	£2,000
5	£1,000	**5**	£1,000
4	£500	4	£500
3	£300	3	£300
2	£200	2	£200
1	£100	1	£100

SCORE SHEET

contestant's name	contestant's name
....	....

50:50	📞	👥	50:50	📞	👥
☐	☐	☐	☐	☐	☐

15	£1 MILLION	15	£1 MILLION
14	£500,000	14	£500,000
13	£250,000	13	£250,000
12	£125,000	12	£125,000
11	£64,000	11	£64,000
10	£32,000	10	£32,000
9	£16,000	9	£16,000
8	£8,000	8	£8,000
7	£4,000	7	£4,000
6	£2,000	6	£2,000
5	£1,000	5	£1,000
4	£500	4	£500
3	£300	3	£300
2	£200	2	£200
1	£100	1	£100

SCORE SHEET

contestant's name	contestant's name
....	....

50:50	☎	👥	50:50	☎	👥
☐	☐	☐	☐	☐	☐

15	£1 MILLION		15	£1 MILLION
14	£500,000		14	£500,000
13	£250,000		13	£250,000
12	£125,000		12	£125,000
11	£64,000		11	£64,000
10	£32,000		10	£32,000
9	£16,000		9	£16,000
8	£8,000		8	£8,000
7	£4,000		7	£4,000
6	£2,000		6	£2,000
5	£1,000		5	£1,000
4	£500		4	£500
3	£300		3	£300
2	£200		2	£200
1	£100		1	£100

SCORE SHEET

contestant's name	contestant's name
....	....

50:50 ☎ 👥   50:50 ☎ 👥

☐ ☐ ☐   ☐ ☐ ☐

15	£1 MILLION	15	£1 MILLION
14	£500,000	14	£500,000
13	£250,000	13	£250,000
12	£125,000	12	£125,000
11	£64,000	11	£64,000
10	£32,000	10	£32,000
9	£16,000	9	£16,000
8	£8,000	8	£8,000
7	£4,000	7	£4,000
6	£2,000	6	£2,000
5	£1,000	5	£1,000
4	£500	4	£500
3	£300	3	£300
2	£200	2	£200
1	£100	1	£100

SCORE SHEET

<table>
<tr><td>contestant's name
................................</td><td>contestant's name
................................</td></tr>
</table>

50:50	☎	👥	50:50	☎	👥
☐	☐	☐	☐	☐	☐

15	£1 MILLION		15	£1 MILLION
14	£500,000		14	£500,000
13	£250,000		13	£250,000
12	£125,000		12	£125,000
11	£64,000		11	£64,000
10	£32,000		10	£32,000
9	£16,000		9	£16,000
8	£8,000		8	£8,000
7	£4,000		7	£4,000
6	£2,000		6	£2,000
5	£1,000		5	£1,000
4	£500		4	£500
3	£300		3	£300
2	£200		2	£200
1	£100		1	£100

SCORE SHEET

contestant's name	contestant's name
....	....

50:50	☎	👥		50:50	☎	👥
☐	☐	☐		☐	☐	☐

15	£1 MILLION		15	£1 MILLION
14	£500,000		14	£500,000
13	£250,000		13	£250,000
12	£125,000		12	£125,000
11	£64,000		11	£64,000
10	£32,000		10	£32,000
9	£16,000		9	£16,000
8	£8,000		8	£8,000
7	£4,000		7	£4,000
6	£2,000		6	£2,000
5	£1,000		5	£1,000
4	£500		4	£500
3	£300		3	£300
2	£200		2	£200
1	£100		1	£100

SCORE SHEET

contestant's name	contestant's name
....	....

50:50 🕿 👥	50:50 🕿 👥
☐ ☐ ☐	☐ ☐ ☐

15	£1 MILLION	15	£1 MILLION
14	£500,000	14	£500,000
13	£250,000	13	£250,000
12	£125,000	12	£125,000
11	£64,000	11	£64,000
10	£32,000	10	£32,000
9	£16,000	9	£16,000
8	£8,000	8	£8,000
7	£4,000	7	£4,000
6	£2,000	6	£2,000
5	£1,000	5	£1,000
4	£500	4	£500
3	£300	3	£300
2	£200	2	£200
1	£100	1	£100

S C O R E S H E E T

contestant's name	contestant's name
....	....

50:50	☎	👥		50:50	☎	👥
☐	☐	☐		☐	☐	☐

15	£1 MILLION		15	£1 MILLION
14	£500,000		14	£500,000
13	£250,000		13	£250,000
12	£125,000		12	£125,000
11	£64,000		11	£64,000
10	£32,000		**10**	£32,000
9	£16,000		9	£16,000
8	£8,000		8	£8,000
7	£4,000		7	£4,000
6	£2,000		6	£2,000
5	£1,000		**5**	£1,000
4	£500		4	£500
3	£300		3	£300
2	£200		2	£200
1	£100		1	£100

SCORE SHEET

contestant's name	contestant's name
....	....

50:50 ☎ 👥	50:50 ☎ 👥
☐ ☐ ☐	☐ ☐ ☐

15	£1 MILLION	15	£1 MILLION
14	£500,000	14	£500,000
13	£250,000	13	£250,000
12	£125,000	12	£125,000
11	£64,000	11	£64,000
10	£32,000	**10**	£32,000
9	£16,000	9	£16,000
8	£8,000	8	£8,000
7	£4,000	7	£4,000
6	£2,000	6	£2,000
5	£1,000	**5**	£1,000
4	£500	4	£500
3	£300	3	£300
2	£200	2	£200
1	£100	1	£100

SCORE SHEET

contestant's name	contestant's name
....	....

50:50	☎	👥		50:50	☎	👥
☐	☐	☐		☐	☐	☐

15	£1 MILLION	15	£1 MILLION
14	£500,000	14	£500,000
13	£250,000	13	£250,000
12	£125,000	12	£125,000
11	£64,000	11	£64,000
10	£32,000	10	£32,000
9	£16,000	9	£16,000
8	£8,000	8	£8,000
7	£4,000	7	£4,000
6	£2,000	6	£2,000
5	£1,000	5	£1,000
4	£500	4	£500
3	£300	3	£300
2	£200	2	£200
1	£100	1	£100

SCORE SHEET

contestant's name	contestant's name
....	....

| 50:50 📞 👥 | 50:50 📞 👥 |
| ☐ ☐ ☐ | ☐ ☐ ☐ |

15	£1 MILLION	15	£1 MILLION
14	£500,000	14	£500,000
13	£250,000	13	£250,000
12	£125,000	12	£125,000
11	£64,000	11	£64,000
10	£32,000	10	£32,000
9	£16,000	9	£16,000
8	£8,000	8	£8,000
7	£4,000	7	£4,000
6	£2,000	6	£2,000
5	£1,000	5	£1,000
4	£500	4	£500
3	£300	3	£300
2	£200	2	£200
1	£100	1	£100

S C O R E   S H E E T

contestant's name	contestant's name
....	....

| 50:50 | ☐ ☐ ☐ | 50:50 | ☐ ☐ ☐ |

15	£1 MILLION	15	£1 MILLION
14	£500,000	14	£500,000
13	£250,000	13	£250,000
12	£125,000	12	£125,000
11	£64,000	11	£64,000
10	£32,000	**10**	£32,000
9	£16,000	9	£16,000
8	£8,000	8	£8,000
7	£4,000	7	£4,000
6	£2,000	6	£2,000
5	£1,000	**5**	£1,000
4	£500	4	£500
3	£300	3	£300
2	£200	2	£200
1	£100	1	£100

SCORE SHEET

contestant's name	contestant's name
....	....

50:50			50:50		
☐	☐	☐	☐	☐	☐

15	£1 MILLION	15	£1 MILLION
14	£500,000	14	£500,000
13	£250,000	13	£250,000
12	£125,000	12	£125,000
11	£64,000	11	£64,000
10	£32,000	**10**	£32,000
9	£16,000	9	£16,000
8	£8,000	8	£8,000
7	£4,000	7	£4,000
6	£2,000	6	£2,000
5	£1,000	**5**	£1,000
4	£500	4	£500
3	£300	3	£300
2	£200	2	£200
1	£100	1	£100

SCORE SHEET

contestant's name	contestant's name
....	....

50:50 📞 👥👥   50:50 📞 👥👥

☐ ☐ ☐   ☐ ☐ ☐

15	£1 MILLION	15	£1 MILLION
14	£500,000	14	£500,000
13	£250,000	13	£250,000
12	£125,000	12	£125,000
11	£64,000	11	£64,000
10	£32,000	**10**	£32,000
9	£16,000	9	£16,000
8	£8,000	8	£8,000
7	£4,000	7	£4,000
6	£2,000	6	£2,000
5	£1,000	**5**	£1,000
4	£500	4	£500
3	£300	3	£300
2	£200	2	£200
1	£100	1	£100

SCORE SHEET

contestant's name	contestant's name
....	....

50:50			50:50		
☐	☐	☐	☐	☐	☐

15	£1 MILLION		15	£1 MILLION
14	£500,000		14	£500,000
13	£250,000		13	£250,000
12	£125,000		12	£125,000
11	£64,000		11	£64,000
10	£32,000		10	£32,000
9	£16,000		9	£16,000
8	£8,000		8	£8,000
7	£4,000		7	£4,000
6	£2,000		6	£2,000
5	£1,000		5	£1,000
4	£500		4	£500
3	£300		3	£300
2	£200		2	£200
1	£100		1	£100

SCORE SHEET

contestant's name	contestant's name
....	....
50:50 📞 👥👥	50:50 📞 👥👥
☐ ☐ ☐	☐ ☐ ☐

15	£1 MILLION	15	£1 MILLION
14	£500,000	14	£500,000
13	£250,000	13	£250,000
12	£125,000	12	£125,000
11	£64,000	11	£64,000
10	£32,000	10	£32,000
9	£16,000	9	£16,000
8	£8,000	8	£8,000
7	£4,000	7	£4,000
6	£2,000	6	£2,000
5	£1,000	5	£1,000
4	£500	4	£500
3	£300	3	£300
2	£200	2	£200
1	£100	1	£100

SCORE SHEET

contestant's name	contestant's name
....	....

50:50	☎	👥	50:50	☎	👥
□	□	□	□	□	□

15	£1 MILLION	15	£1 MILLION
14	£500,000	14	£500,000
13	£250,000	13	£250,000
12	£125,000	12	£125,000
11	£64,000	11	£64,000
10	£32,000	**10**	£32,000
9	£16,000	9	£16,000
8	£8,000	8	£8,000
7	£4,000	7	£4,000
6	£2,000	6	£2,000
5	£1,000	**5**	£1,000
4	£500	4	£500
3	£300	3	£300
2	£200	2	£200
1	£100	1	£100

SCORE SHEET

50:50

15	£1 MILLION	15	£1 MILLION
14	£500,000	14	£500,000
13	£250,000	13	£250,000
12	£125,000	12	£125,000
11	£64,000	11	£64,000
10	£32,000	10	£32,000
9	£16,000	9	£16,000
8	£8,000	8	£8,000
7	£4,000	7	£4,000
6	£2,000	6	£2,000
5	£1,000	5	£1,000
4	£500	4	£500
3	£300	3	£300
2	£200	2	£200
1	£100	1	£100

SCORE SHEET

<table>
<tr><td>contestant's name</td><td>contestant's name</td></tr>
<tr><td>...................................</td><td>...................................</td></tr>
</table>

50:50 ☎ 👥 ☐ ☐ ☐   50:50 ☎ 👥 ☐ ☐ ☐

15	£1 MILLION		15	£1 MILLION
14	£500,000		14	£500,000
13	£250,000		13	£250,000
12	£125,000		12	£125,000
11	£64,000		11	£64,000
10	£32,000		10	£32,000
9	£16,000		9	£16,000
8	£8,000		8	£8,000
7	£4,000		7	£4,000
6	£2,000		6	£2,000
5	£1,000		5	£1,000
4	£500		4	£500
3	£300		3	£300
2	£200		2	£200
1	£100		1	£100

SCORE SHEET

contestant's name	contestant's name
....	....

50:50	☎	👥	50:50	☎	👥
☐	☐	☐	☐	☐	☐

15	£1 MILLION	15	£1 MILLION
14	£500,000	14	£500,000
13	£250,000	13	£250,000
12	£125,000	12	£125,000
11	£64,000	11	£64,000
10	£32,000	**10**	£32,000
9	£16,000	9	£16,000
8	£8,000	8	£8,000
7	£4,000	7	£4,000
6	£2,000	6	£2,000
5	£1,000	**5**	£1,000
4	£500	4	£500
3	£300	3	£300
2	£200	2	£200
1	£100	1	£100

SCORE SHEET

contestant's name	contestant's name
....	....

50:50	☎	👥		50:50	☎	👥
☐	☐	☐		☐	☐	☐

15	£1 MILLION	15	£1 MILLION
14	£500,000	14	£500,000
13	£250,000	13	£250,000
12	£125,000	12	£125,000
11	£64,000	11	£64,000
10	£32,000	**10**	£32,000
9	£16,000	9	£16,000
8	£8,000	8	£8,000
7	£4,000	7	£4,000
6	£2,000	6	£2,000
5	£1,000	**5**	£1,000
4	£500	4	£500
3	£300	3	£300
2	£200	2	£200
1	£100	1	£100

S C O R E   S H E E T

contestant's name	contestant's name
....	....

50:50	☎	👥		50:50	☎	👥
☐	☐	☐		☐	☐	☐

15	£1 MILLION	15	£1 MILLION
14	£500,000	14	£500,000
13	£250,000	13	£250,000
12	£125,000	12	£125,000
11	£64,000	11	£64,000
10	£32,000	10	£32,000
9	£16,000	9	£16,000
8	£8,000	8	£8,000
7	£4,000	7	£4,000
6	£2,000	6	£2,000
5	£1,000	5	£1,000
4	£500	4	£500
3	£300	3	£300
2	£200	2	£200
1	£100	1	£100

SCORE SHEET

contestant's name		contestant's name	
....		....	

50:50	☎	👥		50:50	☎	👥
☐	☐	☐		☐	☐	☐

15	£1 MILLION		15	£1 MILLION
14	£500,000		14	£500,000
13	£250,000		13	£250,000
12	£125,000		12	£125,000
11	£64,000		11	£64,000
10	£32,000		**10**	£32,000
9	£16,000		9	£16,000
8	£8,000		8	£8,000
7	£4,000		7	£4,000
6	£2,000		6	£2,000
5	£1,000		**5**	£1,000
4	£500		4	£500
3	£300		3	£300
2	£200		2	£200
1	£100		1	£100

Calling all
Who Wants To Be A Millionaire? Junior fans!

Younger players can now experience the real tension and excitement of being a contestant and host of their favourite game show with.......

Who Wants To Be A Millionaire? Junior Board Game

Based on the No.1 hit game show.
For ages 8-12, and 2-5 players or teams, each player takes it in turn to act as host while the other players try to win more and more money by answering fun questions using their own hand-held display modules.

It's time to beat the adults with your own game!

Enjoyed
Who Wants To Be A Millionaire? Junior
Want to up the stakes?
Then try one of the family quiz books…

Are you one of those addicted viewers who
can't get enough of *Who Wants To Be A Millionaire?*

Do you sweat it out in the hot-seat of your
armchair as much as the contestants on screen?

Now you can pull your hair out over the thousands of tormenting
teasers in all these: *Who Wants To Be A Millionaire? The Quiz
Book*, *The Ultimate Challenge* and *The Bumper Quiz Book*.

Compiled in the same easy-to-play format including the
Fastest Finger First round, the 50:50 Lifeline and an audience
you can ask at any time, day or night, these *Who Wants To Be
A Millionaire?* quiz books provide a chance for all would-be
contestants to pit their wits against the show's question
masters and battle it out for the £1,000,000 jackpot.

So get your fastest finger ready – are you up to the challenge?

Available from all good bookshops

The publishers would like to thank the
following for their help in producing this book:

Harry Nicholas Adams

Joe Adams

Sam Bailey

Tom Bailey

Jordan Brown

Stephanie Erin Cockburn

Molly Dodwell

Holly Hope Fletcher

Olivia Gregorian

Megan Jones

Sam Jones

Kitty Hannah Keating

Djamela Magid

Alexandra Matthews

Rosanne Eve McKernan

Dario Pase

Jessica Louise Patterson

Simon Asheley Patterson

Sophie Pisano